THE WAY WE WERE

*How Southern Baptist Theology
Has Changed and What It Means
To Us All*

FISHER HUMPHREYS

MCCRACKEN PRESS

NEW YORK

McCracken Press™

An imprint of Multi Media Communicators, Inc.

575 Madison Avenue, Suite 1006
New York, NY 10022

Library of Congress Cataloging-in-Publication Data:

Humphreys, Fisher.
    The way we were: how Southern Baptist theology has changed and what it means to us all / Fisher Humphreys
            p.   cm.
    Includes bibliographical references.
    ISBN 1-56977-588-5: $12.95
    1. Southern Baptist Convention—Doctrines.
2. Baptists—Doctrines. 3. Church controversies—Baptists—History—20th century. I. Title.
BX6462.7.H86 1994
230'.6132—dc20   94-17726
                                        CIP

10 9 8 7 6 5 4 3 2 1

Printed in the United States of America

Contents

To Dr. and Mrs. S. B. Platt,
and to the First Baptist Church
of Columbus, Mississippi,
who first taught me
the theology of the Southern Baptists

Preface

For a decade and a half the Southern Baptist Convention has been convulsed by a tragic controversy which has inflicted appalling suffering upon tens of thousands of good people on both sides of the aisle. The conflict has generated impassioned speech, as indeed it should; passion about the controversy is natural, appropriate, and necessary. But it is not sufficient. I made the decision to attempt to write dispassionately about the theological issues in the controversy because I felt that I was losing sight of the trees in my passion for the forest and that others might be having the same experience. Who are the Southern Baptists? What do they believe? How are they changing? These are the questions I attempt to answer in this book.

I am indebted to my friend Bill Griffin for his encouragement while I was writing this book and for his help in arranging for its publication.

Four other friends read a somewhat earlier version of the book, Paul Basden, Timothy George, John Loftis, and Philip Wise. They provided enormously helpful suggestions, and I am grateful to them all. Of course, the responsibility for any remaining misjudgments or asperities is mine.

I am dedicating this book to my home church, which in the space of only four years managed to instill in me as a teenager a profound respect, which has lasted for four decades, for the theological heritage of the Southern Baptists. After I had left Columbus, the men's Sunday School classes in the church made it possible for me to do graduate studies in theology which I could never have done without their help, and my life took a turn which it otherwise might not; I am deeply grateful to them all. I am dedicating the book in particular to one couple in the church, Dr. and Mrs. S. B. Platt, who helped me to understand the inner meaning of the Baptist theological heritage, especially its commitment to missions, by the way they lived as well as by the things they said. They cannot know how much they contributed to my life.

In essentials, unity.
In non-essentials, liberty.
In all things, charity.

—Rupertus Meldenius[1]

INTRODUCTION:

A Fading Heritage

THE SOUTHERN BAPTISTS

In 1990, there were approximately 250 million people living in the United States. The largest religious body in the country is the Roman Catholic church, with approximately fifty-five million members. The second largest is the Southern Baptist Convention, with approximately fifteen million members.

The fifteen million Southern Baptists are members of approximately 38,000 churches. While the center of gravity for Southern Baptists is still the Old South, churches affiliated with the Convention are to be found in all fifty states and in the District of Columbia.

Southern Baptists operate the largest religious publishing house in the world, the Sunday School Board, in Nashville. The Sunday School Board, in turn, owns and operates 55 bookstores, the largest chain of religious bookstores in the nation. Southern Baptists have two mission boards, one for missionaries abroad and one for missionaries in the United States, with a total of approximately 8,000 missionaries under appointment. The Convention owns six seminaries, including three of the four largest accredited seminaries in the world, with a total enrollment of about 10,000 students.

The operations of the national organization constitute only a part of what Southern Baptists are doing. The 38,000 churches also are organized into forty state conventions, and many of these own and operate institutions of their own. For example, the various state conventions own forty-five colleges and universities, including large, well-known universities such as Baylor, Richmond, Wake Forest, Mercer, Stetson, and Samford.[2]

Although the growth rate of Southern Baptists has slowed in recent years, the Convention is still growing more rapidly than other large Protestant denominations in this country. Of denominations with more than a million members in the United States, only the Assemblies of God are growing faster than the Southern Baptists.

But all is not well with the Southern Baptists. Since 1979, they have been engaged in a controversy. As a result, the Southern Baptists are polarized into two groups, and many of the leaders of Southern Baptist agencies before 1979 have been replaced by new leaders. Even the naming of the two groups has been a matter of controversy. Those who approve of the new directions in the Convention tend to refer to the new leaders as "conservatives" and to the old leaders as "liberals." Those who disapprove of the new directions tend to call the new leaders "fundamentalists" and the old leaders "moderates" or "conservatives."

The two groups do agree on one matter, however; they agree that Southern Baptists will never again be exactly the kind of people they were before the controversy. That is the premise upon which this book is being written: The Southern Baptists are changing and will not become again exactly the people they were before 1979. My primary purpose in writing this book is to record and interpret the beliefs that the Southern Baptists held in the years just before the controversy began. I intend the book to be an archive of the way we were, theologically. My subsidiary purpose is to track the directions in which theology is moving in the new Southern Baptist Convention.

What is the Relevance of this Archive?

Future historians who study American Christianity may well welcome a record of the beliefs which the Southern Baptists held before the controversy changed them, but is there anyone now who needs such a record? I believe there is. We who are Southern Baptists are finding it difficult to interpret exactly what is happening to us, and one reason is that our memory of who we once were is beginning to fade. Like people in a small boat sailing farther and farther from shore, we can no longer see the shoreline well enough to be certain where our journey began, so we are unable to interpret where we now are and where we are going. Our origin should be for us a fixed point, so that we can better understand what is happening to us.

The changes in the theology of the Southern Baptists are also relevant to people who are not Southern Baptists. For example, in the years leading up to 1979, Southern

Baptists were enthusiastic supporters of a rigorous separation of church and state. Like many Americans, they were at first puzzled by the Supreme Court decisions in the 1960s which stated that state-sponsored prayers in public schools constituted a violation of the no-establishment clause of the First Amendment, but many Southern Baptists quickly came to see that these decisions were consistent with the longstanding Baptist support for complete government neutrality toward religion. The new leaders of the Southern Baptists have indicated, however, that they do not see things that way. The Southern Baptist change of direction on this issue is important to all Americans.

I hope that this book will help readers understand what Southern Baptists once believed, so that they may understand better the changes going on in the Convention, and how the new Southern Baptist Convention is different from the Convention before 1979.

Is an Archive Possible?

Scholars who study religions routinely expect to find several factors in the religions they study. Among these are a cult, a code, and a creed. A cult is a set of worship practices. A code is a set of moral rules. A creed is a set of beliefs, a worldview.

The Southern Baptist Convention may therefore be expected to have these three. This book is about the third factor, the beliefs of the Southern Baptists. What worldview do these fifteen million people share?

Some readers may be surprised to learn that the conventional wisdom among many of the scholars who study the Southern Baptist Convention has been that it is not possible to provide a description of the theological beliefs of Southern Baptists.

Three objections have been offered to the attempt to delineate the theology of the Southern Baptists. The first objection is that Baptists in general, and Southern Baptists in particular, have no written creed. Without a creed, the argument goes, we cannot know what the people believe.

It is true that Southern Baptists do not have a creed. But they do have a confession, entitled *The Baptist Faith and Message*. Adopted by the Convention at the annual meeting in 1963, it is a very useful description of the beliefs of Southern Baptists. It also has been much debated in the controversy.

A second argument used by those who believe that it is not possible to describe the theology of the Southern Baptists, appeals to a famous Baptist slogan, "No creed but the Bible."[3] Since Southern Baptists are committed to the Bible as the source of their beliefs, the argument goes, the only possible description of their beliefs is the Bible itself.

The premise is true, but the conclusion does not follow. Once again, the argument overlooks an important fact, namely, that Southern Baptists believe that the Bible teaches some particular things. We here stipulate that throughout this book our description of the theology of the Southern Baptists is, in fact, a description of what the Southern Baptists believe the Bible teaches, for the Southern Baptists certainly think that their beliefs are biblical beliefs.

Finally, some scholars have felt that the beliefs held by

fifteen million Southern Baptists are too diverse to be susceptible of a single description. Folk wisdom expresses this with a slogan: "Where there are two Southern Baptists, there are three opinions." Once again, the premise is true but the conclusion does not follow. Let us here stipulate that great diversity of beliefs exists among the Southern Baptists. But along with the diversity, there is great unity. In the present book we shall describe and interpret the unity and the variety of the beliefs of the Southern Baptists.

Is There a Need for This Archive?

Even though they have no creeds, Baptists[4] have left a paper trail which may be followed by those who wish to discern the shape of their theology. In view of that paper trail, is there any need for a book such as this one? My conviction is that there is a need, because of the nature of the paper trail.

The trail is very large and very scattered. We have already noted that it includes *The Baptist Faith and Message*. It also includes the hymnal entitled *Baptist Hymnal*. Of course, Southern Baptists are not required either to believe *The Baptist Faith and Message* or to sing from the *Baptist Hymnal*, but, in fact, they do believe what is in the confession and they do use the hymnal.

The paper trail includes many other books also. For example, in 1977 the Church Training Department of the Sunday School Board initiated a new study for the churches, called the Doctrine Study. Each year, a Southern Baptist author writes a book on a particular doctrine, and the book is widely distributed and studied in the churches.[5] The authors include pastors, denominational leaders, missionaries, and professors at colleges and seminaries. These books are a useful record of the theology of Southern Baptists. Another set of books which is a bridge between the work of academic theologians and the consensus theology of the people is the sixteen-volume *Layman's Library of Christian Doctrine*, written by Southern Baptist pastors and professors.[6]

The paper trail includes books of systematic theology and biblical theology which have been written by professional Southern Baptist theologians.[7] It also includes all of the following: curriculum materials which have been prepared for Sunday School and other church programs; articles which have appeared in the four theological journals published by the seminaries;[8] the many theological editorials and articles which have been published in the thirty-nine newspapers which are published by the state conventions; and the numerous articles, books, and doctoral dissertations which have been written on the theology of Southern Baptist individuals and groups.[9]

A distinction needs to be made between the consensual theology of the people and the intentional, creative reworking of that consensus by professional theologians. Our interest here is more with folk theology than with academic theology, with what is lived out in church, home, and marketplace rather than with what is written by scholars. Southern Baptist theologians stay extremely close to the concerns of the people in the churches, closer perhaps than is the case with theologians in other denominations, but they also are responsive to the concerns of the academic discipline of theology as well, as indeed they should be.[10]

Unfortunately, there are not any detailed, scientific surveys about the beliefs of Southern Baptists upon which to draw, though sociologist Nancy Ammerman has done some work of this type.[11] It is regrettable that no oral history of Southern Baptist folk theology has been recorded.[12]

Another source for understanding the theology of the Southern Baptists is their practices. For example, Southern Baptist churches baptize by immersion, not by pouring or sprinkling. No written record of this practice would be found in, for example, the *Baptist Hymnal,* yet the uniform practice makes it clear that Baptists believe in this mode of baptism, and it is appropriate to take the practice as evidence for the belief.

The present book is needed because the paper trail is large and dispersed. The shape and texture of the theology of the Southern Baptists are fading and will fade from our memories; this retrieval of our fading heritage is offered to our children as a patrimony and to ourselves as a reminder of the way we were.

Interpreting the Controversy

The Southern Baptist Convention is a large and complex organization, and the controversy that began in 1979 is a large and complex social dislocation. Many interpretations of the Southern Baptist controversy have been offered. This is a good thing. Because the controversy is complex, many interpretations are needed.[13] We do not err when we accept several interpretations; we err when we assume that a single interpretation tells us everything that is important. For example, some well-intentioned interpreters have suggested that the controversy is "really" about political power; it is about political power, both inside and outside the Convention, but it is not about political power alone.

The interpreter also should not assume that theology is a smoke screen to cover up other unmentionable issues such as sexism or racism; this seems to be the thesis of one recent study.[14] The problem with such a thesis is that it is unfalsifiable; nothing counts against it. When dealing with empirical matters one should be able to state with some precision what empirical data count against a proposed interpretation.

The most helpful interpretations of a complex social movement such as the controversy in the Southern Baptist Convention acknowledge the complexities of the movement, attend to the complexities, report them all with some fullness, and attempt to show the relationships among them. It is reductionism of the most egregious kind to assert that the theology of the Southern Baptists is "really" a cover for racism or sexism. This is like saying that romantic love is "really" only about sex or that capital punishment is "really" only about revenge.

Several major kinds of interpretation of the controversy are needed. For example, the controversy needs to be interpreted historically.[15] It also needs to be interpreted sociologically.[16] It also needs to be understood in terms of the personalities who have led in the changes and those who have resisted it.[17]

Interpreters who emphasize the history, sociology, and personalities of the controversy will give attention to many factors, including the expansion of Southern Baptists beyond the Old South; the cultural changes in the Old South; the civil rights movement and the response of the Old South; the changing role of women in America; the development of Southern Baptist bureaucracies; the growth of the financial base of the Southern Baptists; the changes in American political life and the place of Southern Baptists in those changes; the culture wars in America; the increasing influence of television upon church life; the worldwide resurgence of religious movements which bear family resemblances to this one;[18] and many other factors.

To the interpretations of the controversy which emphasize history, sociology, and personalities, I want to add an interpretation which emphasizes theology. From the beginning of the controversy in 1979, the new leaders of the Convention have insisted that theology is one of their central concerns. I know of no reason to suppose either that they are insincere or that they are mistaken about their own intentions, and, in that sense, the controversy clearly is about theology. Furthermore, after a decade and a half it seems clear to many observers that, as a matter of fact, theology has been a factor in the controversy. Theology is an issue in the controversy, an important issue, though not the only issue. But is theology the most important issue in the controversy? It is for some people, but other issues are more important for other people. This differs from one person to the next. Our assumption is simply that this complex social dislocation called the controversy comprises many important components and that one of them is theology.

The Organization of This Book

This book is not a history of the theology of the Southern Baptists.[19] Nor is the format of the present book a sequence of theological themes.[20] Nor is the present book simply a review of beliefs which are peculiar to Baptists.[21]

This book has three parts. The first is a review of the majority tradition which was accepted by most Southern Baptists up until the controversy began. It is the *consensus fidelium*, the understanding which these believers share about God and the world and their place in the world.

The second part is a review of six alternative agendas which have been offered to Southern Baptists, which significant minorities of Southern Baptists have accepted. These agendas could be called the *diversitas fidelium*, the diversity to be found among these believers.

The third part is an effort to interpret what is happening to the majority tradition of Southern Baptists as a result of the changes in the Convention since 1979. The new majority tradition could be called the *revisio fidelium*, the revised beliefs of the majority of the new Convention.

The majority tradition is described in Chapters one through four. In Chapter 1 we review the beliefs which Southern Baptists share with all the Christians in the world. In Chapter 2 we consider the beliefs which Southern Baptists share with Protestant Christians. In Chapter 3 we review the beliefs which Southern Baptists share with other Baptists. And in Chapter 4 we examine the beliefs which Southern Baptists share with the churches which have accepted the orientation to Christianity which was developed during the great revivalist movement of the eighteenth century.[22]

The sequence here is chronological: a description is given of the beliefs of groups which originated in the first century, in the sixteenth century, in the seventeenth century, and in the eighteenth century, respectively.

Six alternative agendas are proposed by minorities among Southern Baptists. These are described in Chapters 5 through 10. They also are dealt with in chronological sequence.

The first alternative agenda is the Anabaptist agenda, the agenda which the more radical wing of the Reformation proposed to the church. The second is the Calvinist agenda. The first two minority agendas originated in Europe in the sixteenth century. The third is the Landmark Baptist agenda. This is a distinctly American agenda which was developed during the nineteenth century. The fourth is the deeper life agenda; this agenda was developed in Great Britain and America late in the nineteenth century. The fifth is the fundamentalist agenda. This is a distinctively American agenda and was developed early in the twentieth century as a response to liberal Protestant theology. The sixth is the progressive agenda. Unlike the others, it is not a group of interrelated beliefs, but rather several discrete proposals which have been offered to Southern Baptists since the middle of the twentieth century.

The third section comprises two chapters. The first describes which of the majority beliefs held in the years leading up to 1979 are at risk in the new Southern Baptist Convention. The second describes which of the beliefs which were held by minority groups in 1979 are becoming part of the majority tradition in the new Convention.

PART ONE

THE MAJORITY TRADITION

CHAPTER 1

Beliefs Baptists Share with All Christians

The followers of Jesus Christ in the world today are to be found in hundreds of churches and denominations, and the initial impression which an observer gets of them is one of variety to the point of dissipation. An interested bystander might well ask, "Do these people share any common beliefs?"

Even if we discover that they do, will not these beliefs be, so to speak, a lowest common denominator, a collection of ideas which are agreed upon only because they are so trivial that no one cares enough about them to disagree with others about them?

These natural assumptions are held by many people who observe the churches casually and by some who study the churches carefully. But they should not be held, for they are not true. In fact, the beliefs which are held by all the churches are religiously the most indispensable and theologically the most profound. These universal Christian beliefs may be summarized by considering eleven themes.

There Is One God

Jews, Christians, and Muslims agree concerning the first of these beliefs, namely, that there is only one true God.

There were brushes with monotheism before it became the cardinal doctrine of the Hebrews. Ikhnaton promoted it in Egypt, and in the fourth century before Christ some Greek philosophers came to see that the Ultimate Reality must be one rather than many. What is remarkable is not that these precursors of monotheism arose, but that they failed, and that monotheism as held by the Jews succeeded so fully that it now is an operating assumption for Western philosophy and theology and has credibility even in some Eastern religions. For example, in the West there is a vigorous discussion of the arguments for and against the existence of God; there is no discussion of arguments for or against the existence of gods. In Hinduism, to take another example, many intellectuals such as the late philosopher and president of India, Sarvepalli Radhakrishnan, believe that the many gods and avatars of Hinduism are different names for a single Deity.

Monotheism has not always been so dominant. When Israel became monotheistic, she was alone and her neighbors thought she was foolish. Her neighbors asked, "Where is your God?" (Psalm 115:2).

Not surprisingly, scholars have disagreed about exactly when the Hebrew people became monotheists. Some have thought that monotheism was the original belief of humankind and that polytheism was a later corruption.

Others have seen Abraham as the first monotheist. Others have asserted that Moses was the first monotheist, in part because the Shema is attributed to him: "Hear, O Israel, the Lord our God is one Lord" (Deut. 6:4). More critical scholars have argued that monotheism did not come into its own until the great prophets of the eighth and seventh centuries before Christ.[23]

Our interest here is not with the chronology of monotheism but with the fact that the conviction that there is only one true God became the cardinal belief of the Hebrews.

From the beginning, monotheism was fully accepted by all Christians. It is true that the Christian doctrine of the Trinity goes beyond Hebrew monotheism, but it is an addition, not a rejection. The Shema is quoted in the New Testament (Mark 12:2), always with approval, and some of the early Christian confessions of faith such as Ephesians 4:4-6 assert that there is only one God.

Monotheism is one of the great success stories of the Jewish and Christian religions. Most people in the West find it unnecessary to affirm the conviction that there is only one true God; this is a belief which is assumed rather than affirmed or defended. This is as true of Baptists as it is of all other Christians. *The Baptist Faith and Message* (II) says simply: "There is one and only one living and true God."

God Created the World

The second belief which Baptists share with all other Christians is the belief that God created the world. Like monotheism, this belief has become part of the thinking

of almost all Western people. Ask people in the West,
"What do you think of when I say the word 'God'?" and
most will respond, "The One who made the world."

Yet it is by no means self-evident that God created the
world. Other relationships between God and the world
are, in principle, quite possible. For example, Plato
taught that the world is eternal as God is, and God mere-
ly molds a world which He did not create. The Stoics
taught that the world is God's body, and God is the soul
of the world. Some Gnostics taught that the world was
created by a being other than God.

Christians, like Jews and Muslims, believe that God is
the creator of the world because this truth is revealed in
the Bible. The placing of the story of Creation at the very
beginning of the Bible, Genesis 1-2, reinforces the importance of the idea. The Hebrew Scriptures contain other
passages which affirm that God is creator, such as Job
38-39, Psalm 104, and Isaiah 45:9-12. The New Testament
reaffirms Creation when it says that God's Word "brings
into being what did not exist" and when it tells us that "it
is by faith that we understand that the universe was created by God's word, so that what can be seen was made out
of what cannot be seen (Rom. 4:17, Heb. 11:3).

In the ancient world, the affirmation that God is creator of all things was an alternative to views which originated in other religions. In the early history of the
church, the belief that God is creator was an alternative to
views which originated in philosophy. In the modern
world, belief in God as creator has been presented as an
alternative to views which originate in science.

Because of the different stances which Christians take
toward the issue of how God created the world, it is easy

to lose sight of the universal agreement among Christians that God is the creator of all things. In particular, Christians disagree among themselves about the accounts of the age of the universe which some scientific theories offer, and they disagree about whether to accept scientific hypotheses concerning the evolution of life on this planet. These differences are important, but it is much more important that, however much Christians may disagree about how God created the world, there is no disagreement about the fact that God created the world.

The universal agreement that God created the world is, of course, shared by Southern Baptists. *The Baptist Faith and Message* (II) says that God is the "Creator, Redeemer, Preserver, and Ruler of the universe." Southern Baptists sing praise to "the King of Creation" who "o'er all things so wondrously reigneth," and they are confident that "This is my Father's world."

Since God created human beings, that means that human beings are good. The Creation story in Genesis speaks of five ways in which human beings are unique: human beings are created last, they are created in God's image, God breathes into them the breath of life, they are given dominion over the rest of the creation, and after God created human beings he said that it was "very good." There may be no more finer passage in all of literature about the dignity of human beings than is found in Psalm 8:

> When I look at the sky, which you have made,
> at the moon and the stars, which you set in
> their places—
> what is man, that you think of him;

mere man, that you care for him?

Yet you made him inferior only to yourself;
you crowned him with glory and honor.
You appointed him ruler over everything you
    made;
you placed him over all creation.

The World Is a Fallen World

The story of the fall of the world into sin, like the
story of the creation of the world, is placed early in the
Bible (Genesis 3), and that has contributed to sin's being
a dominant theme in the theology of Christians. What
Genesis affirms by the memorable story of the Garden of
Eden, the Bible reaffirms many times by the stories of
the sins and failures of individuals, of the nation Israel,
and of the Christian church. Perhaps no other narratives
in the world are so candid about the failures of their central personalities as are those in the Bible; except for Jesus
himself, every major character in the Bible is presented
"warts and all," and the emphasis often falls on the warts.
The Bible also affirms the sin of the human race in more
analytical terms, in passages such as Romans 1-2.

The Christian church has inherited this realistic vision
of the human predicament and has affirmed it repeatedly.
It is a vision which is sometimes resented by people as too
gloomy and pessimistic, and perhaps there have been
times when the church emphasized the grimness of the
human predicament to the neglect of Christian hope.
But the realism of the Bible about sin is very reassuring to
those who wonder if it is possible to be realistic about the

human problem and still retain hope.

Christians have interpreted the sin problem in different ways. In Israel the great prophets such as Amos encountered people who worried too much about the details of the cultic law and too little about the great issues of the moral law, and Jesus found himself in controversy with people who kept the letter but violated the spirit of the law. Both those issues continue today, and others have surfaced in the church's history.

But despite the variety of interpretations, there is considerable agreement among Christians about the human predicament. For example, Christians see the source of the human problem, not in ignorance, suffering, or death, but in sin. Here is how *The Baptist Faith and Message* (III) expresses it:

> By his free choice man sinned against God and brought sin into the human race. Through the temptation of Satan man transgressed the command of God, and fell from his original innocence; whereby his posterity inherit a nature and an environment inclined toward sin, and as soon as they are capable of moral action become transgressors and are under condemnation.

As this quotation makes clear, Southern Baptists are aware of the social dimension of sin. However, they tend to emphasize the personal aspect of sin more than the social; sin is fundamentally an act of moral disobedience to the law of God, which brings upon the sinner the righteous judgment of God. One of the Baptists' favorite hymns, "Amazing Grace," speaks of the human predicament in this way:

Amazing grace! How sweet the sound
That saved a wretch like me.
I once was lost, but now am found,
Was blind, but now I see.

One of the most extraordinary achievements of Christian doctrine is its success in balancing the belief that human beings are good because they are created by God with the belief that they are hopelessly lost in sin. This subtle combination of ideas is held, not only by intellectuals in the church, but by unschooled Christians, even by children.

The balance between these two beliefs has practical implications. For example, is the Christian understanding of human beings optimistic or pessimistic? Is it realistic or idealistic?

It is optimistic because it affirms that the world is God's good creation and that human beings are the crowning work of God's creation, made in God's own image, only a little lower than God himself. It also is realistic rather than idealistic, because it affirms that the world is hopelessly fallen away from its true destiny, and that human beings are enslaved by evil powers and forces, both internal and external, from which they cannot deliver themselves. Blaise Pascal captured well the irony of the Christian vision of human beings when he wrote:

What sort of a freak then is man! How novel, how monstrous, how chaotic, how

paradoxical, how prodigious! Judge of all
things, feeble earthworm, repository of
truth, sink of doubt and error, glory and
refuse of the universe! Who will unravel
such a tangle?[24]

Yet, the final Christian word is one of hope rather
than despair, for the Christian message is an affirmation
that God does for sinners what they cannot do for themselves; he rescues them from their sin.

God is Father, Son, and Holy Spirit

The word *Trinity* does not occur in the Bible, nor does
it occur in *The Baptist Faith and Message*, but the
Trinitarian understanding of God is presented in both.
The second article of *The Baptist Faith and Message* is
entitled simply "God," and it comprises three parts:
"God the Father," "God the Son," and "God the Holy
Spirit." These categories may seem scholastic to outsiders, but they are living realities to Southern Baptists as
well as to other Christians.

In fact, the religious life of Christians is probably more
Trinitarian than their theology. Christians worship and
believe in God, whom they think of and pray to as the
Father of Jesus Christ and as their own heavenly Father.
They also are religiously committed to Jesus as Lord and
Savior, in whom they have placed their faith and hope for
salvation. They also very much believe in the Holy Spirit
as the presence of God with the church and with individual Christians and know that his work is indispensable to
their faith and life.

Baptists, like all Christians, are Trinitarian in their religious life. *The Baptist Faith and Message* makes this fact clear, while displaying the reticence to speak directly about the Trinity which also is characteristic of the Bible.

Yet Baptists do speak about the Trinity directly. For example, they proclaim as gospel the story of the crucifixion and resurrection of Christ; they say that Christ thereby reconciled sinners to God; and they teach that those who accept this gospel receive the gift of the Holy Spirit. Also, they follow the baptismal formula of Matthew 28:19-20 and baptize "in the name of the Father, and of the Son, and of the Holy Spirit." These verses are a favorite text of Southern Baptists and are often referred to as "The Great Commission." Again, Baptists sing the more than fifteen hymns and doxologies in the *Baptist Hymnal* which are Trinitarian. Some of these devote one verse each to the Father, Son, and Spirit. Here, for example, are the opening words of the first four verses of one popular hymn: "Come, thou Almighty King / Come, thou Incarnate Word / Come, Holy Comforter / To thee, great One in Three." Baptists certainly know what the word "Trinity" means, and some of them have definite ideas about the Trinity. Nevertheless, the strength of their commitment to the Trinitarian understanding of God is measured, not by their articulation of their belief, but by its recurrence in the practices of the churches such as Gospel preaching, baptism, and the singing of hymns.

The Father Sent His Son into the World

The fifth belief which Baptists share with all Christians is sometimes called "Incarnation" and is discussed in terms of "Christology." Baptists tend not to use these two terms frequently. They employ much more frequently the biblical language of the Father "sending" his Son into the world. It is almost certainly the case that the most loved verse in the Bible among Baptists is John 3:16: "For God so loved the world that he gave his only-begotten Son."

Baptists recognize that the coming of the Son of God into the world is surrounded by mystery, but they accept, as the Christian church always has, that his mysterious coming was by means of a virgin mother. This fact is celebrated unself-consciously in Christmas carols and in Christmas pageants in Baptist churches each year; it has never been seriously debated among Southern Baptists. Baptists do not share the devotion to Mary which many other Christians have, but they share the belief of all other Christians that Mary was a virgin.

Most Southern Baptist churches do not employ creeds as a part of their liturgy, and many Southern Baptist people are not familiar with the Apostles' Creed.[25] It is interesting to notice, therefore, that *The Baptist Faith and Message* (II) employs the language of the Apostles' Creed when speaking of the birth of Christ. It says: "In His incarnation as Jesus Christ he was conceived of the Holy Spirit and born of the virgin Mary."

Jesus Lived, Preached, Taught, Loved, Died, and Rose Again, to Save the World

Jesus Christ stands at the center of the Christian faith. The four gospels are stories about his life and work. The Gospel message is the story of his death and resurrection.

Here is how the apostle Paul summarizes the gospel:

> I passed on to you what I received, which
> is of the greatest importance: that Christ
> died for our sins, as written in the
> Scriptures; that he was buried and that he
> was raised to life three days later, as writ-
> ten in the Scriptures. (1 Cor. 15:3-4)

Baptists love the story of Jesus, as all Christians do.
They confess their faith in it in *The Baptist Faith and
Message*, and they sing about it in hymns such as "One
Day," "Tell Me the Story of Jesus," and "Victory in
Jesus."

> I heard about his healing,
> Of his cleansing power revealing,
> How he made the lame to walk again
> And caused the blind to see;
> And then I cried "dear Jesus,
> Come and heal my broken spirit,"
> And somehow Jesus came and brought
> To me the victory.

For Baptists as for Paul, the emphasis falls upon the
death and Resurrection of Christ rather than upon his life
and teachings, but the stories of his life and teachings are
loved and told over and over by Baptists. Baptists preach
that Christ died and rose again to save sinners; this message of salvation through Christ is the central feature of
Baptist preaching. *The Baptist Faith and Message* (II)
says: "In his death on the cross He made provision for the
redemption of men from sin." The created world is a

stage on which the drama of redemption is acted out, and the story of Jesus is the center of that drama. The optimism of the Baptist message originates, not in any observations about the world or general theories about progress, but in the conviction that "God was in Christ, reconciling the world unto himself" (2 Cor. 5:19, KJV).

The Father and the Son Poured Out the Holy Spirit on the Church

In Acts 2 Luke tells the story of God giving his Holy Spirit to the disciples of Christ on the Day of Pentecost. The gift of the Spirit fulfilled several prophecies in the Hebrew Scriptures and also fulfilled promises which Jesus had made to his disciples.[26] When the Spirit was given, the church was born. One of God's most precious gifts to his church is his presence with them as Holy Spirit.

Baptists believe in the Holy Spirit. *The Baptist Faith and Message* (II) lists sixteen activities of the Spirit. The Spirit enables people to understand the Bible, cultivates Christian character, comforts believers, gives spiritual gifts to Christians, protects and assures Christians, and enlightens and empowers the Christian and the church in worship, evangelism, and service.

Baptists sing about the Spirit less frequently than they do about Christ, but their hymns include prayers for the power, cleansing, enlightenment, and comfort of the Spirit. Most Southern Baptists have avoided the Pentecostal and charismatic movements, but they nevertheless believe very deeply in the presence and work of the Spirit.

The Spirit Guides and Empowers the Church on its World Mission

The Christian church is a missionary church. It was born to do missionary work, as the Book of Acts emphasizes. Southern Baptists love to emphasize this aspect of the church's work. Missions is the raison d'etre of Southern Baptists. Those who founded the Southern Baptist Convention thought of themselves as

> organizing a plan for eliciting, combining, and directing the energies of the whole denomination in one sacred effort, for the propagation of the Gospel.[27]

Baptists sing about missions. "We've a Story to Tell to the Nations," they sing. They tell their youth that their responsibility with reference to the Gospel is to "Pass it on."

More than seventy percent of the money given through the central funding agency of the Southern Baptist Convention, called the Cooperative Program, is given to the two mission boards. Further, two very large offerings are taken in the churches each year, one at Christmas for foreign missions and one at Easter for missions work in the United States; together they amount to more than one hundred million dollars a year. Southern Baptists are serious about missions, and their commitment to missions has been the strongest bond holding them together across the decades.

Baptists recognize that, for all their plans and all their energy and commitment, the success of the missionary enterprise depends on God's blessing it, and they know that God's blessing is given through the Holy Spirit who guides and empowers the church in this work. It is the Holy Spirit who "calls men to the Saviour, and effects regeneration" (*Baptist Faith and Message*, II).

The Church Preaches the Gospel and Observes the Ordinances of Christ

From its inception, the Christian church was a preaching church. Peter preached on the Day of Pentecost, and Acts records sermons preached by Stephen and by Paul. The content of the apostolic preaching was the kerygma, the message that Christ had died and risen again to bring salvation. The church is a community of memory which never forgets what happened on Good Friday and Easter Sunday.

The Christian church is reminded of the momentous events of Jesus' life, not only by its preachers, but by its observance of two symbolic acts. These acts are baptism and the Lord's Supper. From its inception, in obedience to commands given by Christ, the church baptized and observed the Lord's Supper.[28]

Southern Baptists believe in preaching, and they believe in baptism and the Lord's Supper.

Most Southern Baptist churches have three services each week, two on Sunday and a third on Wednesday evening, with a sermon as part of each one. Many churches still follow the traditional practice of setting aside one or more periods of time each year for special revival preaching. Many Baptists also listen to other preaching, either on the radio or television or by visiting neighboring churches which are engaged in special services. Preaching is an important factor in the life of Southern Baptists.

Baptists get their name from one of the two principal church ordinances; *ordinance* is the name which Southern Baptists ordinarily use for what are called "sacraments" in most churches, namely, baptism and the Lord's Supper. Surprisingly, however, Southern Baptists tend not to think of the observance of the ordinances as a component in the mission of the church. Rather, they think of the observance of the ordinances as acts of obedience to Christ which the church observes when the primary work of preaching, evangelizing, and missions has been carried out. The phrase *Word and Sacrament*, which is so accurate a description of the life of many churches, is a little misleading as a description of the life of Southern Baptists; though both components are found in Southern Baptist life, Baptists see preaching as the carrying out of the church's mission and the ordinances as obedient acts of remembering the crucified and risen Lord.

God Will Complete His Work in the Future

From its inception Christianity was a religion of hope. The earliest Christians had been trained to hope by their Jewish faith, and Jesus had given them a reason to hope by means of his message and his Resurrection from the dead. Christians look not only to a past in which God has acted in history but to a future in which God will complete history. They think of God as pushing them from behind, as with them in the present moment, and as waiting for them in the future.

Southern Baptists share the hope which has characterized the life of the church from the beginning. Generally
they speak of this hope in terms of heaven; there are eigh-
teen hymns in the *Baptist Hymnal* about heaven. Some
of the titles are "We're marching to Zion," "O that will be
glory for me," "When we all get to heaven," and "Face to
face with Christ my savior."

The Baptist Faith and Message says simply: "The righteous in their resurrected and glorified bodies will receive
their reward and will dwell forever in Heaven with the
Lord."

Baptists believe that salvation includes many things,
and they can speak eloquently of these things. To be saved
is to find a meaning for life; it is to find a true Friend,
Jesus Christ; it is to be forgiven of your sins; it is to become
part of the family of God. But most of all, to be saved is
to have your eternal destiny changed from hell to heaven.
Evangelistic preaching often takes the form of warnings
about hell, and heaven figures much larger in Baptist theology than even the numerous hymns might suggest.

Baptist hope is not restricted to heaven; Baptists have
ideas about the future of life on this planet. They hold
diverse ideas about this, so *The Baptist Faith and
Message* (X) appropriately says quite neutrally that "God,
in His own time and in His own way, will bring the
world to its appropriate end."

The diversity of beliefs about how the world will end
should not distract our attention from the more fundamental fact, which is that Baptists share with all
Christians the conviction that they are entitled to live in
hope because the future belongs to God just as the past
and the present do.

The Bible Tells us this Wonderful Story

The Bible is the holy book of the Christian church. The earliest Christians treasured the Hebrew Scriptures, in which they found many passages which helped them to understand God's great work of sending Jesus Christ and pouring out the Spirit. Soon Christians began to write their own books, and, under the leadership of God, they collected them and eventually recognized them as also being the Word of God, authoritative for the faith and life of the Christian community.

Baptists are proud to be a people of The Book, the Bible. They owe their existence to the efforts of women and men in the seventeenth century who felt that it was important to leave the Church of England in order to form a church which would be more faithful to the New Testament. Baptists study the Bible, read the Bible, teach the Bible, preach the Bible, argue about the Bible, and write about the Bible. They even sing about the Bible: "Holy Bible, book divine, precious treasure, thou art mine." In the summer study program called Vacation Bible School which Baptists conduct for children, the children usually participate in a pledge to the American flag, a pledge to the Christian flag, and a pledge to the Bible.

Baptists share the conviction of all Christians that the Bible is the Word of God. Baptists love the Bible because, as a beloved hymn says,

> Beyond the sacred page,
> I seek thee, Lord
> My spirit pants for thee,
> O living Word.

The Bible has the "wonderful words of life" which Baptists need and which they proclaim to all who will listen.

The Baptist Faith and Message (I) affirms clearly the convictions of Baptists about the Bible, that it is God's Word, that it is uniquely inspired, and that it is authoritative for the faith and life of the church.

> The Holy Bible was written by men divinely inspired and is the record of God's revelation of Himself to man. It is a perfect treasure of divine instruction. It has God for its author, salvation for its end, and truth, without any mixture of error, for its matter.

Since 1979 Southern Baptists have been engaged in a controversy about the Bible. But the controversy has not been about any of the ideas mentioned here: that the Bible is God's Word, that it is uniquely inspired, and that it is authoritative for the faith and life of the church. The controversy has been about a more technical issue than these, and we will deal with that issue in chapter nine. For now, it is important to note that the Bible is the holy book for Baptists as it is for all Christians and that Baptists, like other Christians, regard it as God's Word and as the written authority for the faith and life of the church.

These, then, are eleven beliefs which Southern Baptists hold in common with all of the world's Christians, whether Protestant, Catholic, or Orthodox: There is one God; God created the world; the world is fallen; God is

Father, Son, and Spirit; the Father sent his Son into the world; Christ lived and died and rose again to save the world; the Father and the Son gave their Spirit to the church; the Spirit guides and empowers the church on its world mission; the mission includes preaching and the ordinances; God will complete his work in the future; and the Bible tells us this wonderful story.

The conventional name for these beliefs which all Christians share is "Christian orthodoxy." They are what has been believed everywhere, always, by everyone in the church.[29]

Southern Baptists are orthodox Christians.[30]

These eleven beliefs are the most important beliefs which Baptists hold. Instead of being a lowest common denominator, they are a highest common denominator. What unites Baptists and other Christians is far more important than what divides them.

Yet all Christians do not share this judgment. In fact, the center of gravity in the faith and life of many Southern Baptists lies, not in what has been described in this chapter, but in some of the beliefs which will be described in Chapter 4. Nevertheless, the beliefs described in this chapter are the indispensable background for those revivalist beliefs.

CHAPTER 2

Beliefs Baptists Share with Protestant Christians

Baptists have sometimes debated whether or not they are Protestants. One popular version of their history is that Baptist churches, or at least proto-Baptist churches, existed throughout the history of the church. However, the consensus among historians today is that the Baptist movement was born among Puritans who separated from the Church of England very early in the seventeenth century. The first Baptist church was founded in 1608 or 1609 by English citizens living in Holland. Since Baptists came into existence about three quarters of a century after the great Reformation of the sixteenth century, it is natural to ask what beliefs Baptists share with Protestants. There are five of these.

The Church Must Always Seek to be Reformed

The New Testament presents the church as the body of Christ, as the bride of Christ, and as a holy nation.[31]

The Roman Catholic church has understood these and other New Testament images to mean that the church is indefectible. That is, while individual church members and leaders may and do commit sins and make mistakes, the church itself, as Christ's body, cannot sin or make mistakes. Some isolated factors in the church's life may be in error, but the great direction of the church cannot err because it is Christ's body through which he lives and works in the world; it is his bride without spot or blemish.

This is a very reassuring doctrine, and it is understandable that the Roman Catholic church came to believe it. Nevertheless, Martin Luther, John Calvin, Ulrich Zwingli, John Knox, and the other great reformers rejected it. What they saw led them to believe that the church was defectible rather than indefectible. They thought that the church not only could err but had erred, in that it had misled people about the Gospel of Christ. In place of the idea that the church is defectible, the reformers put another idea: *Ecclesia semper reformanda*, the church must always be being reformed. Later theologians such as Paul Tillich have called this "the Protestant principle." It means that the church should never claim infallibility for itself, but should always humbly seek to know God's will better and to be more devoted to God.

Baptists accept the Protestant principle. They do not believe that the church is indefectible. Instead, they speak consistently of the need of the church to be more committed to Christ and more faithful to His calling. The terms which they use for this are "revival" and "renewal." Baptists are open to a revival of the life and commitment of God's people because they know that the church is very imperfect. The church must never claim indefectibility for itself but must always seek humbly to be reformed in ways that draw it closer to God's will.

The Bible Alone is the Written Word of God

As is stated in Chapter 1, all Christians believe that the Bible is the Word of God. This is as true of Roman Catholics as of Protestants. During the centuries when the Roman Catholic Church was the only church in the West, it came to believe in two sources of revelation, that is, that the official teaching of the church given through councils and creeds, and interpreted by the magisterium or teaching authority of the bishops and Popes, is the Word of God just as the Bible is.

The Protestant reformers rejected this idea of church tradition as a second source of revelation. Of course, they did not reject everything that had been said by councils and in creeds. For example, John Calvin's great book, *The Institutes of the Christian Religion*, was an extended commentary on the Apostles' Creed which had been used in the Roman Catholic Church for more than a thousand years.

What Protestants rejected was the notion that the authority of the church, the councils, the creeds, and the Pope, was on a par with the authority of the Bible. The Protestant position was summarized in the phrase, *sola Scriptura*, the Bible alone is the Word of God. Perhaps the most famous story about this is the story of Martin Luther at the Diet of Worms saying that he would never renounce the things he had written unless he were shown from Scripture that he was mistaken.

The Protestant emphasis on Scripture is a very influential belief in Baptist life. Baptists love the Bible, and they are totally sympathetic with its having priority over all other written documents. In fact, Baptist church members rarely study any document other than the Bible, and when they do study other documents, it is with the understanding that these are not authoritative in the way the Bible is. *The Baptist Faith and Message* preface says, "The sole authority for faith and practice among Baptists is the Scriptures of the Old and New Testaments."

Justification is by Grace through Faith Alone

What Martin Luther learned from his study of the Bible was that efforts to save oneself by prayers, good works, and so on, are not only doomed to fail but are in conflict with the Christian understanding of salvation as a free gift of God. The reformers retrieved the language of the apostle Paul: "We conclude that a person is put right with God only through faith, and not by doing what the Law commands (Rom. 3:28)." Protestants call this principle *sola fide*, which means one is saved "by faith alone."

Baptists accept *sola fide*. In the nineteenth century, this principle led them to separate from some persons, who went on to form the Churches of Christ, over the question of whether or not baptism was essential to salvation. As important as baptism is to Baptists, they were persuaded that to insist that baptism is essential to salvation is to violate the principle of *sola fide*, and they refused to do that.

When the reformers spoke of salvation, their preferred terminology was the legal idea of justification or acquittal before God; for Southern Baptists, the preferred terminology has come to be regeneration, the new birth into the family of God; of course, both groups have used both terms. The new birth occurs when an individual responds to the convicting work of the Holy Spirit with repentance and faith. *The Baptist Faith and Message* (IV) says:

> Repentance and faith are inseparable experiences of grace. Repentance is a genuine turning from sin toward God. Faith is the acceptance of Jesus Christ and commitment of the entire personality to Him as Lord and Saviour.

Southern Baptists sing many hymns which reflect their commitment to the principle of *sola fide*.

> At the cross, at the cross,
> Where I first saw the light,
> And the burden of my heart rolled away
> It was there by faith
> I received my sight,
> And now I am happy all the day.

They urge those who are not yet Christians:

> Only trust him, only trust him,
> Only trust him now;
> He will save you, he will save you,
> He will save you now.

They use phrases such as "coming home," "turn your eyes upon Jesus," and "I will arise and go to Jesus" to speak of what the reformers called *sola fide*, putting one's faith in Jesus as one's savior and Lord. Southern Baptists know quite well that this response to Christ results in salvation only because God is a God of grace.

> Grace, grace, God's grace,
> Grace that will pardon and cleanse within; Grace, grace, God's grace,
> Grace that is greater than all our sin.

All Believers are Secure in Their Salvation

The Roman Catholic church teaches that it is possible for Christians to forfeit their salvation either by egregious sin or by apostasy in belief. John Calvin and his successors denied that possibility. Southern Baptists share Calvin's conviction that those who are Christians will not forfeit their salvation. *The Baptist Faith and Message* (V) is emphatic about this:

> All true believers endure to the end. Those whom God has accepted in Christ, and sanctified by his Spirit, will never fall away from the state of grace, but shall persevere to the end. Believers may fall into sin through neglect and temptation, whereby they grieve the Spirit, impair their graces and comforts, bring reproach on the cause of Christ, and temporal judgments on themselves, yet they shall be kept by the power of God through faith unto salvation.[32]

The hymns which Baptists sing confirm this view. No hymn in the *Baptist Hymnal* hints at the possibility of apostasy, and many confirm the security of God's children.

> My faith has found a resting place
> Not in device or creed;
> I trust the ever living One,
> His wounds for me shall plead.
> I need no other argument,
> I need no other plea,
> It is enough that Jesus died,
> And that he died for me.

In one favorite hymn, God speaks these words to his people:

> The soul that on Jesus hath leaned for repose
> I will not, I will not desert to his foes;
> That soul, though all hell should endeavor to
> shake, I'll never, no, never, no, never forsake!

All Believers Are Priests of God

The biblical message concerning priests is fascinating. The priests of the Hebrew Scriptures were elite male descendants of Levi and later of Aaron, but the Hebrew Scriptures also contain two passages which prophesy a coming time when all of God's people will be priests (Gen. 19:5-6, Isa. 61:5-6). The New Testament says that those prophecies are fulfilled in the Christian church; I Peter 2:4-10 is the most explicit text, and Christians are called priests in five passages in Revelation.

Prior to the Reformation of the sixteenth century, the Western church did not emphasize the priestly work of all Christians. Instead, priestly work was reserved for a male elite, the clergy of the church. This became a sign of the oppression of the people by their leaders, and it was rejected by Martin Luther and the other reformers. Luther reaffirmed the priesthood of believers in his book *The Freedom of the Christian Man* and elsewhere. It was an idea whose time had come.

In the New Testament, the priesthood of believers was a way of speaking of the privilege and responsibility of all Christians to do things such as surrender their lives as sacrifices to God and do good works as sacrifices to God.[33]

For Luther, the priesthood of all believers was a symbol for freedom as well as for privilege and responsibility. Since Luther, the priesthood of believers has been called upon to support the proposals which Christians make in the name of "the glorious freedom of the children of God" (Rom. 8:21).

Understood as a symbol for Christian freedom, the priesthood of all believers is well represented in *The Baptist Faith and Message* (VI and XVII). Of the church that document says: "In such a congregation members are equally responsible," and of religious liberty it says: "A free church in a free state is the Christian ideal." It also says: "Baptists emphasize the soul's competency before God, freedom in religion, and the priesthood of the believer."

The reference to "the soul's competency" calls for some explanation. The champion of that phrase was the most creative of Southern Baptist theologians, E. Y. Mullins.

In a book entitled *The Axioms of Religion: A New Interpretation of the Baptist Faith*, first published in 1908, Mullins defined soul competency as the freedom, ability, and responsibility of each person to respond to God for himself or herself. He argued that it is the most distinctive and important of Baptist beliefs, and that it is the "mother principle" from which six axioms may be derived. The theological axiom is that God has the right to be sovereign. The religious axiom is that all persons have a right to access to God. The ecclesiastical axiom is that all believers have a right to equal privileges in the church. The moral axiom is that only a free soul is a responsible soul. The religiocivic axiom is a free church in a free state. The social axiom is, "You shall love your neighbor as yourself." Mullins's use of the word "right" makes it clear that he is speaking throughout of freedom. What the phrase "priesthood of believers" affirms for Christians, Mullins's phrase "soul competency" affirms for all human beings.

These, then, are five beliefs which Southern Baptists share with Protestants but not with Roman Catholics: The church should always be in the process of being reformed; the Bible alone is the Word of God; salvation is by God's grace through faith alone; all believers are secure in their salvation; and all believers are priests before God.

Interestingly, the Roman Catholic Church may be having second thoughts about some of these traditionally Protestant beliefs. The Second Vatican Council, which met from 1962 until 1965, seems to have set aside, or at least to have minimized, the two-source theory of revelation, and many Roman Catholics now speak quite freely of "the priesthood of all the faithful." Perhaps someday

Baptists will hold these beliefs in common with Roman Catholics as well as with Protestants. In any case, these are part of the Southern Baptist theological heritage.

CHAPTER 3

Beliefs That are Unique to Baptists

Southern Baptists are part of a worldwide family of Baptists estimated to include about seventy million people. Baptists share many things in common which, at least in the seventeenth century, were found almost exclusively among Baptists. In America today, however, some of these Baptist distinctives have come to be accepted by large numbers of people, including some who are not even church members.

The Baptist distinctives are what many people tend to associate especially with Baptists, and that is understandable. These are important beliefs to Baptists. Throughout this book, however, we have been insisting that to understand Baptists one must observe not only what is distinctive to Baptists but what they hold in common with other Christian groups.

The distinctively Baptist beliefs are all related to the two general ideas of church life and freedom. We shall describe them in terms of eight themes.

Only Believers Should be Baptized

From its inception, the Christian church has practiced a rite of initiation which employs water and which is called "baptism." Until the formation of the Society of Friends (Quakers) in the sixteenth century, no church existed which did not practice baptism.[34] All of the churches agreed that baptism was an act of obedience to Christ and that it was to be done "in the name of the Father, and of the Son, and of the Holy Spirit" (Matt. 28:19-20).

The first persons to be baptized were adults(Acts 2:37-41). It is unclear exactly when Christians began to baptize infants. Doubtless it seemed a natural practice to people who were familiar with the Hebrew practice of circumcising male infants. We do know that in the fourth century Augustine developed the theory that baptism eradicates original, inherited sin, and the acceptance of this theory insured that the baptism of infants would continue.

In any case, it was a dramatic moment in the history of the Christian church when a group of English men and women in Amsterdam, under the leadership of John Smyth, renounced the baptism which they had received as infants as no baptism at all, and submitted to baptism as adult believers. In 1608 or 1609 Smyth baptized himself first, and then the members of his congregation, thereby forming the first Baptist church.

Southern Baptists have retained the view that only believers should be baptized. They do not baptize their infants, nor do they count them as members of the church. They do enroll them in Sunday School classes and other organizations, and they teach them the Bible and nurture them in the Christian heritage, but until children are old enough to take the step of faith, they are not baptized. This helps explain why so much of the preaching in Southern Baptist worship services is evangelistic; there always are non-church members present, even if only the children of the members.

In recent years Southern Baptists have tended to baptize more and more children at a very early age, sometimes as young as five years or even younger. However, this represents a revision of the understanding of the age at which it is possible for persons to come to faith on their own rather than a retreat from the principle of believers baptism.

Given the distinctiveness of their belief about baptism, it is surprising to learn that Baptists do not sing very much about baptism.[35] Nor is a great deal of space given to baptism in *The Baptist Faith and Message* (VII), which says simply, "Christian baptism is the immersion of a believer in water in the name of the Father, the Son, and the Holy Spirit." Commitment to believers baptism is so deeply embedded and implicit in Baptist life and thought that it does not need to be made explicit very often.[36] To the best of my knowledge, no Southern Baptist church has ever baptized an infant.

Believers baptism was originally a practice peculiar to the Baptists, but that is no longer the case. Other denominations such as the Disciples of Christ and the Assemblies of God practice believers baptism. What was once a Baptist distinctive has become part of the heritage of a wider family of Christians.

Baptism is by Immersion Only

Baptists have two beliefs about baptism which set them apart from other Christians. One is that the only proper candidates for baptism are believers; the other is that the only proper mode of baptism is immersion. Baptists believe that baptism is proper only when it is biblical, and it is biblical only when believers are immersed.

All churches permit immersion as a mode of baptism, but what is distinctive about Baptists is that, beginning about the middle of the seventeenth century, they disallowed any mode other than immersion. It is not certain when or why Christian churches had come to practice a mode other than immersion in the first place. Perhaps it was done very early, and perhaps the motivation was simply convenience. In any case, Baptists felt that to be true to the New Testament, the church must immerse believers fully, and that is what they did. By the 1640s immersion was the routine practice of the little Baptist churches in England, and it is the routine practice of Baptists today. Several other denominations in America have followed the Baptists in this practice.

The Church Consists of Believers Only

Prior to the Reformation, everyone born in the West was baptized into the Roman Catholic Church, except those infants whose parents refused to allow them to be baptized, parents such as Jews or, in Southern Spain, Muslims. Church and society were, for all practical purposes, the same people. But many sincere people came to long for something else; they longed to be a part of a community of faith in which all members were intentionally committed to Christ.

The Reformation did not change that situation; the principle adopted at the Reformation was *cuius regio, eius religio*, that is, the official religion of a country would be the religion adopted by the prince of that country. The ruler might grant greater or less tolerance to dissenters, but, except for the dissenters, the members of the church were the citizens of the nation. The Reformation did not satisfy the desire which many people felt to belong to a community of intentionally committed people of faith, a believers church.

The Puritans who separated from the Church of England were moving toward a believers church, but because they continued to baptize their children, their churches also comprised both intentional believers and those who were not yet intentionally committed. The Baptists took the next logical step when they restricted baptism to believers, thereby forming communities comprising only intentional believers. It was the fulfillment of the desire which many people had held for many centuries.

In the United States today, the idea of a believers church seems natural not only to Baptists but to virtually all Americans. Historian Martin Marty has spoken of the "baptistification" of American religion, by which he means the widespread acceptance among Americans of the idea that the only genuine religion is that which one accepts for oneself.[37]

The Baptist Faith and Message (VI) defines a church as follows:

> A New Testament church of the Lord
> Jesus Christ is a local body of baptized
> believers who are associated by covenant
> in the faith and fellowship of the gospel..

The ideal of a believers church, like that of believers baptism by immersion, is assumed in Southern Baptist life more often than it is affirmed or defended. The Baptist conviction that churches should be intentional communities of faith is most evident in the Baptist practice of restricting baptism to those with faith in Christ.

Each Congregation is Self-Governing

Once the Baptists had established themselves in the seventeenth century as believers churches independent of the established Church of England, they faced the question of how they would be governed. The decision was made to follow the practice of their older cousins, the Congregationalists. Rather than to look to outsiders such as bishops or synods to make decisions concerning congregational life, each congregation was to govern itself.

To understand the question of church government, also known as church order, it is necessary to recognize that the debates center around how to find the will of God for the church. No Christians have ever defended the idea that churches are entitled to do whatever they, or their bishop, or their synod, decide to do. The different forms of church government are, in fact, efforts to discern the mind of Christ for the church.

Fundamentally there are three forms of church government.[38] One is oligarchy, which is government by a small, self-perpetuating group within the church; this form of government is practiced in the Roman Catholic Church. The second is representative government, which is government by a small, elected group within the church; this form is practiced in the Presbyterian Church. The third is democratic government, which is government by all of the members of the group; this form is practiced in Congregational churches and in Baptist churches.

Of course, all three forms get modified in practice. Nevertheless, these three forms of church government propose a fundamentally different understanding of where the decision-making power resides in the church.

All three have appealed to the New Testament for their justification. In some ways, Paul behaved like a bishop toward the churches to whom he wrote his letters; that justifies the Episcopal form of government. Again, the first century synagogues elected elders to govern them, and it is likely that the early churches did the same; that justifies the Presbyterian form of government. Finally, Paul appealed to the church members at Corinth and elsewhere, rather than to their bishops or pastors or elders, to correct the problems in their common life; that justifies the Congregational form of government.

Today many scholars doubt that the New Testament writers intended to provide instructions about how the church is to be governed. Many would agree with Eduard Schweizer: "There is no such thing as *the* New Testament church order."[39] While the proponents of the various views understandably appeal to the New Testament in support of their views, the fact is that the New Testament does not instruct Christians on precisely how to govern themselves. Paul would have needed only a few verses to tell Timothy exactly how a church should be governed, but he did not do so, and the result is that different forms of church government have developed across the years.

When the first Baptists adopted the congregational form of church government, they had a pattern to follow, that of the churches of the Congregationalists. The pattern worked well, and it has been followed ever since. Southern Baptist congregations make decisions about all manner of things, confident that no person or group outside the congregation has any power over the congregation. The congregation may look outside for advice if it chooses to do so, but it is the church members, not outsiders, who in the end make the decisions for the congregation.

As might be expected, Southern Baptists do not sing about this idea, and even *The Baptist Faith and Message* (VI) is brief to the point of being cryptic: "This church is an autonomous body." In the seventeenth century, autonomy was not self-evidently a good idea, but it has worked well for almost four centuries. Today many other denominations have joined Baptists and Congregationalists in founding self-governing congregations.

All Members Share in the Church's Decision Making

Once it is established that local congregations are to be self-governing, how are they to do that? The Baptist answer is that they do it democratically. Each member participates equally in the decision making.

Some people do not like to use the term "democratic" of Baptist congregations. They point out that, in a democracy, voters are obliged to ask only what they want, whereas in Baptist churches, members are obliged to ask what they believe Christ wants. The distinction is a useful one, and it is reflected in *The Baptist Faith and Message* (VI) which says that a congregation operates "through democratic processes under the Lordship of Jesus Christ." To this it immediately adds: "In such a congregation members are equally responsible."

Whether or not the term "democratic" is used, the issue is clear. Granted that pastors and others exercise great authority and leadership in a church; granted that many decisions will be referred to committees and to other groups and individuals; granted that the ideal is to seek consensus rather than for a majority to abuse a minority in the church; still the question remains, "In the final analysis, who makes the decisions for the congregation?" And the Baptist answer is, "Under the Lordship of Jesus Christ, the people themselves, by democratic procedures."

Congregations Should Cooperate with Each Other

Upon learning that each Baptist congregation is self-governing, one might assume that the congregations would have little or no relationship with each other. In principle, that is possible, but in practice, it is not the case. From the beginning, Baptist congregations have cooperated with each other to discuss ethics and doctrine, to do ministries of education and benevolence, and, especially among Southern Baptists, to do missionary work.

The cooperation of the congregations is never coerced, however; it is always voluntary. Among Southern Baptists, there are regional associations, state conventions,

and the national Southern Baptist Convention with
which congregations may voluntarily associate themselves, but no one forces any Baptist congregation to associate or to cooperate.

The primary motivation for cooperation among
Southern Baptists is practical rather than theological. It
is not so much that the congregations believe in Christian
unity in a way that requires them to cooperate among
themselves, but rather that they know that they cannot
successfully carry out the work of missions effectively
unless they cooperate. The founding document of the
Southern Baptist Convention says that the Convention
was being organized to allow the churches to do missions
together; the Baptists meeting in Augusta in 1845 said
that they were

> organizing a plan for eliciting, combining,
> and directing the energies of the whole
> denomination in one sacred effort, for the
> propagation of the Gospel.[40]

The Baptist Faith and Message (XIV) picks up some of
the language of that document to affirm the appropriate-
ness of cooperation among the congregations. In an article entitled "Cooperation" we read:

> Christ's people should, as occasion
> requires, organize such associations and
> conventions as may best secure coopera-
> tion for the great objects of the Kingdom
> of God. Such organizations have no
> authority over one another or over the
> churches. They are voluntary and adviso-

ry bodies designed to elicit, combine, and
direct the energies of our people in the
most effective manner.

One great leader of Southern Baptists, Grady Cothen,
has commented that on paper the Southern Baptist
Convention will not work. It is a shrewd observation.
Since cooperation among the 38,000 churches is entirely
voluntary, and since no person or group outside each
congregation has any authority to compel the cooperation
of the congregations, it is difficult to see, in principle,
how the congregations could ever get anything done.

Nevertheless, the Convention has been a very efficient
organization. The reason is that Southern Baptists trust
one another and feel loyalty to the Convention, and their
trust and loyalty lead them to cooperate voluntarily and
enthusiastically. They meet together, they share in common work, they own institutions such as the mission
boards, they pray for one another, they accept members
from each other's churches, and they bear one another's
burdens. All of this is done voluntarily. It is facilitated
by the great denominational service organizations such as
the Woman's Missionary Union and the Sunday School
Board, but local congregations who draw upon the
resources provided by these agencies do so quite voluntarily.

Occasionally one hears Southern Baptists complaining
about the huge bureaucracy which has developed. This is
quite understandable. Bureaucracy is a fact of modern
life, and its problems are well-known.[41] Nevertheless,
Baptists prefer bureaucrats to bishops because bureaucrats, unlike bishops, can be ignored with impunity.

Walter Shurden has commented that Southern Baptists

have been one of the most "denominationalized" of people. How did Southern Baptists ever develop so much loyalty to their denomination? Many factors contributed to this loyalty. Most of them live in the South. Many of them attend Southern Baptist colleges and universities and participate in Southern Baptist summer camps. Their ministers attend Southern Baptist seminaries together. They read books and Sunday School lessons by Southern Baptists, and they contribute money to support Southern Baptist missionaries. The number of programs developed and conducted among Southern Baptists is so great that it is unlikely that any individual knows about all of them. For several decades the Convention has been so large that there was little need for anyone to go outside it for much of anything; whatever one's gifts, they could be used within the Convention, and whatever one's interests, they could be developed within the Convention. The Convention became like a universe to Southern Baptists.

Southern Baptists sing about cooperating with each other:

> Blest be the tie that binds
> Our hearts in Christian love;
> The fellowship of kindred minds
> Is like to that above.
> Before our Father's throne
> We pour our ardent prayers;
> Our fears, our hopes, our aims are one,
> Our comforts and our cares.

The cooperation of Southern Baptists with each other has been encouraged in every way except one: it has never been coerced by any authority outside the local congregation.

Church and State are to be Separate

The relationship between church and state is an issue of freedom, evident in the autonomy of local congregations and in the making of decisions by democratic processes.

The Baptist record on church-state relations is a consistent one, and it begins with the earliest Baptists in England. The following summary of the Baptist heritage draws upon a wonderful brief pamphlet by William Estep.[42]

In 1611, Thomas Helwys, a Baptist layman, led part of the Baptist church which had been formed by John Smyth in Amsterdam back to England. In 1612 he wrote a book entitled *A Short Declaration of the Mystery of Iniquity.* He sent a copy to King James with a handwritten dedication in which he said:

> The king is a mortal man and not God, and therefore has no power over the immortal souls of his subjects, to make laws and ordinances for them, and to set spiritual lords over them. If the king have authority to make spiritual lords and laws, then he is an immortal God and not a mortal man.[43]

For this audacious act Helwys was arrested and put in Newgate Prison, and he is thought to have died there by

1616, a martyr for religious liberty.

In 1614, another Baptist layman, Mark Leonard Busher, wrote *Religious Peace: A Plea for Liberty of Conscience* which he dedicated to King James and to Parliament. It is the first book published in the English language which is devoted entirely to the defense of religious liberty.

In America also, Baptists were early champions of religious liberty. Roger Williams was driven out of the Massachusetts Bay Colony by the Puritans there who claimed freedom for themselves but did not extend it to all others. In 1636 he founded what became Providence, Rhode Island, and in 1639 he founded the first Baptist church in the New World at Providence. He drew up a charter for Rhode Island which promised religious liberty for all in the colony; it was granted in 1644. Williams once wrote:

> All the Liberty of Conscience that ever I pleaded for, turns upon these two Hinges: that none of the Papists, Protestants, Jews, or Turks be forced to come to... Prayers or Worship; nor, secondly, compelled from their own particular Prayers or Worship, if they practice any.[44]

As the new nation was being founded late in the eighteenth century, Baptists were working for assurances that it would be a nation with full religious freedom. The father of the Constitution was James Madison, who was an Anglican but had sympathies for the Baptists of Virginia. Madison learned from John Leland, a Baptist pastor, that the Baptists were not happy with the proposed new Constitution because it did not specify that religious liberty would be given to all. Madison promised the Baptists that if they would help him work for ratification of the Constitution in Virginia, he would see to it that the first order of business of the new Congress formed under the Constitution would be to draw up amendments to the Constitution which would be a bill of rights for the people. Leland agreed, Virginia ratified the Constitution, and Madison kept his word; on June 8, 1789, he proposed the Bill of Rights to the Congress. It was ratified by the states late in 1791.

The sixteen opening words of the First Amendment are the most influential words ever written in support of religious liberty: "Congress shall make no law respecting an establishment of religion, or prohibiting the free exercise thereof." They mean that the government will be neutral toward religion, neither supporting it nor inhibiting it. Many interpretations have been offered of the First Amendment, and many arguments have been made concerning it, but the most important truth is that these words have provided Americans with the greatest religious freedom ever enjoyed by any people in the history of the world.

The separation of church and state has worked. In America, the nation has flourished without an official religion, and the church has flourished without the official support of government. Perhaps the success of this freedom in American has been made possible in part because the American people are a religious people. Although it is conventional to assume that the American people are secular, the polls conducted by George Gallup and others make it clear that the United States is the most religious of the developed nations by a considerable margin. One plausible suggestion is that our religious faith provides us with moral values, and moral values make possible the American way of life which includes government neutrality toward religion. In any case, the point is that religious freedom has worked well in America, and Baptists have been champions of it.

Baptists do not sing about religious freedom very much, though the *Baptist Hymnal* includes hymns such as "America the Beautiful," "My Country, 'Tis of Thee," and "The Star Spangled Banner." Baptists have affirmed religious liberty forcefully in *The Baptist Faith and Message* (XVII). The final article of that document is devoted to the topic, and it says, in part:

> God alone is Lord of the conscience, and he has left it free from the doctrines and commandments of men which are contrary to his Word or not contained in it. Church and state should be separate. The state owes to every church protection and full freedom in the pursuit of its spiritual ends.

Baptists have preached about religious liberty. Perhaps the most famous sermon ever preached by a Southern Baptist pastor was delivered by George W. Truett, the pastor of the First Baptist Church of Dallas, on the east steps of the capitol in Washington on Sunday afternoon, May 16, 1920. Dr. Truett spoke of the historic effort of Baptists to secure religious freedom in the colonial period:

On and on was the struggle waged by our Baptist fathers for religious liberty in Virginia, in the Carolinas, in Georgia, in Rhode Island and Massachusetts and Connecticut, and elsewhere, with one unyielding contention for unrestricted religious liberty for all men, and with never one wavering note. They dared to be odd, to stand alone, to refuse to conform, though it cost them suffering and even life itself. They dared to defy traditions and customs, and deliberately chose the way of non-conformity, even though in many a case it meant a cross. They pleaded and suffered, they offered their protests and remonstrances and memorials, and, thank God, mighty statesmen were won to their contention, Washington and Jefferson and Madison and Patrick Henry, and many others, until at last it was written into our country's Constitution that church and state must in this land be forever separate and free, that neither must ever trespass upon the distinctive functions of the other. It was pre-eminently a Baptist achievement.[45]

Americans who have lived all of their lives with religious liberty, with the understanding that religious faith is something one must accept for oneself, and with democracy in public life and in church life, sometimes find it difficult to appreciate what life was like when people did not have these freedoms. But with a little historical imagination, one can perceive that what we now enjoy is a precious gift from courageous, wise people who went before us, and that it is to be appreciated, defended, and handed along to those who come after us.

Baptists Have No Creed but the Bible

Baptists hold to a technical distinction, one which is not found in most other churches, between creeds and confessions.[46] Creeds and confessions often look very much alike. Often they deal with the same subjects and affirm the same things about those subjects.

Nevertheless, the distinction between them is important to Baptists. The fundamental difference is that confessions are descriptive and creeds are prescriptive. Here is how the historian who has collected many of the Baptist confessions expresses it:

> The Baptist Movement has traditionally been non-creedal in the sense that it has not erected authoritative confessions of faith as official bases of organization and tests of orthodoxy. An authority which could impose a confession upon individuals, churches, or larger bodies, has been lacking, and the desire to achieve uniformity has never been strong enough to secure adoption of a fixed creed even if the authority for imposing it had existed. Still, Baptists have recognized the valuable

uses to which confessions of faith might
be put.[47]

Confessions are descriptive statements, and Baptists
have confessions. Confessions describe the beliefs of a
group of Baptists. They are written and adopted to help
Baptists communicate their beliefs to their own children,
to their fellow Baptists, to Christians in other denominations, and to persons who are not Christians. Baptists
have been drawing up confessions ever since Baptist
churches were first formed, very early in the seventeenth
century.

The Southern Baptist Convention did not draw up a
confession when it was organized, in 1845, and for eighty
years no official, written confession was employed by the
Convention. However, in the latter part of the nineteenth century, a Baptist confession called *The New
Hampshire Confession*, which had been composed in
1833, became very influential among many Baptists in
the South. Then, in 1925, the Southern Baptist
Convention adopted its first official confession, in
response to a controversy concerning evolution. The
1925 document was entitled *The Baptist Faith and
Message*, and it was modeled on the then popular New
Hampshire confession. In 1963, the Southern Baptists
were engaged in another controversy, and one of the
responses to it was the revision and adoption of the 1925
document; the 1963 statement was also entitled *The
Baptist Faith and Message*, and it is this statement to
which we have referred throughout this book.

These documents describe the beliefs of the Southern
Baptists who met in conventions in Memphis in 1925

and in Kansas City in 1963. The preface to the 1963 version says of confessions:

> They constitute a consensus of opinion of some Baptist body, large or small, for the general instruction and guidance of our own people and others concerning those articles of the Christian faith which are most surely held among us. . . . We do not regard them as complete statements of our faith, having any quality of finality or infallibility. . . . The sole authority for faith and practice among Baptists is the Scriptures of the Old and New Testaments. Confessions are only guides in interpretation, having no authority over the conscience.

The descriptive character of confessions is very clear here, and it also shows that the use of this confession or of any confession at all is entirely optional for Southern Baptists. Many Southern Baptist churches and church members have never even heard of *The Baptist Faith and Message*, and those who have heard of it are perfectly free to differ with it without thereby being disloyal to the Convention.

Baptists understand creeds to be entirely different from confessions. Where confessions are descriptive, creeds are prescriptive. Creeds are authoritative statements of what one must believe in order to belong to a particular church. Baptists do not have creeds. They insist that the only written authority for Christian life and faith is the Bible. Their motto is: "No creed but the

Bible." *The Baptist Faith and Message* preface describes
Baptists as anti-creedal:

> Such statements have never been regarded
> as complete, infallible statements of faith,
> nor as official creeds carrying mandatory
> authority.

Though the distinction between creeds and confessions may seem to be theoretical, in fact it has important
practical implications. For example, in 1992 the president of the Foreign Mission Board of the Southern
Baptist Convention, Keith Parks, resigned his position.
He stated that he had philosophical differences with
some of the members of the Foreign Mission Board.
Specifically, he stated that he differed with them on the
matter of creeds. Here is what he wrote:

> Our whole convention has moved more
> toward a creedal approach than a confes-
> sional approach with which I am comfort-
> able. Although not a technical definition,
> my own understanding of the difference
> is that we as Baptists traditionally have
> made our <u>confession</u> of faith and said to
> others, "If you agree with this, let's coop-
> erate and move together in a world mis-
> sion effort." The creedal approach says,
> "This is what I believe, and I must exam-
> ine your beliefs before I am sure that we
> can move together."[48]

In summary, Southern Baptists share eight beliefs with other Baptists around the world and with other Christians who have adopted Baptist beliefs. First, only believers should be baptized. Second, they should be baptized by immersion. Third, the result of believers baptism is a believers church. Fourth, each congregation should function autonomously. Fifth, each congregation should follow democratic procedures in its effort to find God's will. Sixth, congregations should cooperate with each other in order to do their work better. Seventh, the Christian ideal is a free church in a free state, which means that government should be neutral toward religion and that church and state should be kept separate. Finally, Baptists have no creed but the Bible; they adopt descriptive confessions but not prescriptive creeds.

CHAPTER 4

Beliefs Shared with Revivalist Christians

The revivalist movement began more or less simulta-neously in England and in the colonies of New England in the 1730s and 1740s. In England the great leaders were John Wesley, George Whitefield, and Charles Wesley, and in New England the great leader was Jonathan Edwards, though Whitefield made eight trips to the American colonies and made a great contribution to "The Great Awakening" in the colonies.

The influence of this movement upon Christianity in America is immense, and the Southern Baptists have been affected by it as much as any group. The center of gravi-ty for the theology of the Southern Baptists lies in the revivalist heritage. In fact, many Southern Baptists find it difficult to imagine a Christian church which does not accept the four beliefs discussed in this chapter.[49]

Every Individual Must be Converted

All Christian churches hold out the possibility of conversion for persons who have no relationship to Christ or to the church. For example, the Roman Catholic Church would welcome the conversion of a Muslim to Christian faith, and the Lutheran church would welcome the conversion of an atheist to Christian faith.

Revivalism, however, takes this a step further and insists that every person must be converted to be a true Christian, even those who have grown up in the church and accepted what was taught them from childhood.

This is difficult for many Christians to accept. They want to know what one is converted from, if one grew up in Christian faith. They ask why it should be assumed that one's faith is not genuine unless one has arrived at it by means of a spiritual crisis. They point out that in the process of confirmation they internalized for themselves the faith that had been affirmed on their behalf when they were baptized as infants. They think of themselves as having come to faith before they were old enough to articulate it, and they are sure that it is no less real for that. They point out that many people who are genuinely in love did not come to love through a crisis, but their love is nevertheless real; and many who hold deeply to moral convictions did not arrive at them by a profound moral crisis, but their convictions are nonetheless real. It follows, then, they argue, that many people can have genuine faith in Christ without experiencing a profound spiritual crisis.

That was not the view of the great revivalist leaders. As they looked out over England and the American colonies in the eighteenth century, they did not see a

Christian people who needed to be more obedient to their God; they saw a people who were not Christians at all and who needed a conversion experience in order to become Christians. It is not enough, they argued, to be born into a Christian home, in a Christian land, taken to church, and baptized and confirmed. One must accept Christ for oneself; one must experience salvation personally.

The revivalist movement transformed the Christian religion in England and in the colonies. No longer was the world divided into parishes and everyone regarded as a Christian and a member of the official church, except those who intentionally opted out. Now every person, even those who were born and brought up in the most devout homes, had to intentionally commit his or her life to Christ in order to be a Christian.

In general, the churches which adopted the revivalist position have flourished in America, and those which have rejected it have not. The great exception is the Roman Catholic Church, which has grown by immigration and a high birth rate rather than by committing itself to revivalism.

Southern Baptists emphasize the conversion experience. This is the center of gravity in their faith and life. For other Christians the center of gravity may be the Trinitarian understanding of God, or the principle of justification by grace through faith alone, or the Scriptures as the Word of God. Southern Baptists believe these things and think they are important, but the greatest emphasis in Southern Baptist life falls upon conversion. To this experience Baptists return again and again in their thinking. Many of their church services are designed to foster this experience in people. For many Baptists the most important distinction among human beings is the distinction between those who have been converted and those who have not.

The Baptist Faith and Message (VI) assumes the necessity of this experience and the validity of the distinction between those who have been converted and those who have not. It says:

> Salvation involves the redemption of the
> whole man, and is offered freely to all who
> accept Jesus Christ as Lord and Saviour.

Baptists sing about the experience of conversion in many popular songs and hymns. "Ye Must Be Born Again," they sing. Southern Baptist churches usually conclude their worship services with an invitation hymn. This hymn provides an opportunity for individuals to register their decisions publicly. The decision may be to join the church, or to request prayer; but the decision which is most emphasized is the decision to become a Christian, to be converted. The hymn which probably is sung more frequently than any other during invitations is "Just As I Am," which says:

> Just as I am, without one plea,
> But that thy blood was shed for me,
> And that thou bidd'st me come to thee,
> O Lamb of God, I come! I come!

Another popular hymn sung during invitations asks:

> Why should we tarry when Jesus is pleading,
> Pleading for you and for me?

Why should we linger and heed not his mercies,
Mercies for you and for me?
Come home, come home,
Ye who are weary come home;
Earnestly, tenderly, Jesus is calling,
Calling, O sinner, come home!

Occasionally one hears discussions among some Southern Baptists of the relationship between the conversion experience and Christian nurture. These discussions are important, but, they do not diminish the importance of the conversion experience but rather attempt to see it the most important moment in a process which began before conversion and continues after it.

The revivalist understanding of conversion did not originate among Baptists. It originated among Anglicans such as John Wesley and among Congregationalists such as Jonathan Edwards. Nevertheless, the Southern Baptists are the principal beneficiaries of this view of conversion. The reason for this probably is the Baptist view of believers baptism. The Methodists, for example, continue to baptize their babies while preaching that all people need to be converted; understandably, for many Methodists the effect of the practice of baptizing infants gradually eclipses the importance of the need for adult conversion. Baptists do not baptize their babies, so the message about conversion flourishes unhindered by their baptismal practice.

All Christians Should be Sure of Their Salvation

The impression which one gets in reading John Wesley's *Journal* is that nothing was more important to

Wesley than to gain an assurance that he truly was a child of God. In his own life he wrestled with this issue, as is well known, until he gained the assurance he sought in May 1738 at Aldersgate in London. Of that experience he wrote:

> In the evening I went very unwillingly to a society in Aldersgate Street, where one was reading Luther's preface to the *Epistle to the Romans*. About a quarter before nine, while he was describing the change which God works in the heart through faith in Christ, I felt my heart strangely warmed. I felt I did trust in Christ, Christ alone for my salvation; and an assurance was given me that He had taken away *my* sins, even *mine*, and saved *me* from the law of sin and death.[50]

The revivalist movement is not understandable apart from this concern for a personal assurance of one's salvation. In revivalist Christianity, it is not enough to have faith that Christ has died for the sins of the world, or even that Christ has died for one's own sins; one must also have faith that one has personally been forgiven and born anew into God's family.

That was the message which John Wesley preached, and it is the message which Southern Baptists continue to preach today. Confidence that one has been saved is an indispensable component of the religious experience of Southern Baptists. It is an experience which is nurtured by the church in various ways. Individuals who feel assured of their salvation are encouraged to speak of it, and those who lack assurance are encouraged to secure it.

Baptists wed this inner assurance of salvation to the outer security of their salvation as discussed in Chapter 2, to give a very powerful message: Christ has died for you; you can be saved; when you are saved, you can be assured that you are saved; and when you are saved, God will protect you so that you will never lose your salvation.

There is an irony in this message. It emphasizes two apparently contradictory beliefs. The free choice of an individual to intentionally trust Christ is paired with the belief that God will not permit you to forfeit your salvation.

But Baptists do not feel the irony. What they feel is the most reassuring message possible: You are, and always will be, a child of God. With such a reassuring message, it is not surprising that Southern Baptists have grown to become the largest non-Catholic body in America.

To people who do not share this heritage, the language of assurance seems to be presumptuous; who is this, after all, who dares to claim certainty about his or her eternal destiny? While Southern Baptists are as capable of presumption as anyone, the fact is that this tradition encourages quite humble people to speak confidently about the assurance they have of their own salvation. In the revivalist tradition, humble people learn to confess their faith in God's mercy by saying, "I know that I will go to heaven when I die."

Baptists express their assurance of salvation in many ways. *The Baptist Faith and Message* (II) says of the Holy Spirit, for example: "His presence in the Christian is the assurance of God to bring the believer into the fulness of

the stature of Christ." Baptists sing, "Blessed Assurance,
Jesus Is Mine," and:

> I know whom I have believed,
> And am persuaded that he is able
> To keep that which I've committed
> Unto him against that day.

Evangelism is the Primary Task of the Church

In Chapter 1 we saw that all Christians believe that the
Spirit guides the church on a worldwide mission. The
revivalist belief about evangelism goes beyond that belief
in two ways. First, the emphasis of the Christian churches
on mission is general and includes other activities along-
side evangelism such as worship, fellowship, education,
and benevolences, whereas in revivalism the highest priority is given to evangelism. Second, revivalist Christians
believe that it is not enough to proclaim Christ; one must
also attempt to persuade people to respond to Christ.
Some Christians think it is wrong to attempt to persuade
people, but persuasion is an indispensable component of
revivalism.

Southern Baptists are committed to the priority of
evangelism, and they are committed to the need for persuasion in evangelism. They hold evangelistic campaigns,
and they conduct workshops, conferences, and study programs on evangelism. They urge the work of evangelism
upon all churches and all individual Christians. They
teach evangelism in their seminaries.

The Baptist Faith and Message (XI) emphasizes the
work of evangelism.

It is the duty and privilege of every fol-
lower of Christ and of every church of the
Lord Jesus Christ to endeavor to make
disciples of all nations. . . . It is the duty of
every child of God to seek constantly to
win the lost to Christ by personal effort
and by all other methods in harmony
with the gospel of Christ.

The *Baptist Hymnal* carries this emphasis forward. In
one hymn Baptists pray:

> Lord, speak to me, that I may speak
> In living echoes of thy tone;
> As thou hast sought, so let me seek
> Thy erring children lost and lone.

They also pray:

> Lord, lay some soul upon my heart,
> And love that soul through me;
> And may I bravely do my part
> To win that soul for thee.

The emphasis on persuasion is clear in a song by
Fanny Crosby:

> Rescue the perishing,
> Care for the dying,
> Snatch them in pity from sin and the grave;
> Weep o'er the erring one,
> Lift up the fallen,
> Tell them of Jesus the mighty to save.

Missions is a Priority for the Church

The modern missionary movement is usually said to have begun in the 1790s. One of the pioneers in that movement was William Carey, an English cobbler and a Baptist, who gave his life in missionary service in India.

The modern missionary movement is a direct product of the revivalist movement, and the emphasis on missions is a direct product of the emphasis on evangelism associated with revivalism. It is not that missions was restricted to evangelism; in fact, church leaders quickly learned that missionary work succeeds best when it includes works of compassion and of education as well as direct evangelism. But it is clear that evangelism was a major goal of the modern missionary movement, and for that reason we here associate the two.

Across the years, the very best way to catch a sense of the heartbeat of Southern Baptists has been to attend a presentation of the Foreign Mission Board; these presentations traditionally have been made on the Wednesday evening when the Convention meets each year in June. As was pointed out earlier, its founding documents say that the Convention was organized as

> a plan for eliciting, combining, and directing the energies of the whole denomination in one sacred effort, for the propagation of the Gospel.[51]

It is not an exaggeration to say that the Convention has had no sufficient reason to exist apart from missions.

In *The Baptist Faith and Message* there are not separate

articles on missions and evangelism, but one article, entitled "Evangelism and Missions." In the *Baptist Hymnal,* there are not two groups of hymns, one on missions, and one on evangelism, but one group, entitled "Evangelism and Missions." The missionary aspect is quite clear in many of them. For example:

> There's a call comes ringing o'er the restless wave,
> "Send the light! Send the light!"
> There are souls to rescue, there are souls to save,
> Send the light! Send the light!
> Send the Light! the blessed gospel light;
> Let it shine from shore to shore!

They urge one another:

> We have heard the joyful sound:
> Jesus saves! Jesus saves!
> Spread the tidings all around:
> Jesus saves! Jesus saves!
> Bear the news to every land,
> Climb the steeps and cross the waves;
> Onward! 'tis our Lord's command;
> Jesus saves! Jesus saves!

They sing unself-consciously,

> We've a story to tell to the nations,
> That shall turn their hearts to the right.

Southern Baptists encourage each other by singing:

O Zion haste, thy mission, high fulfilling,
To tell to all the world that God is Light;
That he who made all nations is not willing
One soul should perish, lost in shades of night.
Publish glad tidings, tidings of peace,
Tidings of Jesus, redemption and release.

In summary, Southern Baptists share four beliefs with others who have been influenced by the great movement of revivalism which began in England and the American colonies in the eighteenth century. First, they believe that every individual must be converted to faith in Christ; growing up in a Christian home or church is no substitute for a personal experience of conversion. Second, all converts can and should have a deep personal assurance that they are saved. Third, evangelism is the most important work of the church. Finally, God calls the church to be a missionary people and to evangelize the world.

PART TWO

THE
MINORITY
TRADITIONS

CHAPTER 5

Anabaptist Beliefs

There are six clusters of beliefs which have been available to Southern Baptists, which significant minorities have accepted, but which before 1979 had not become part of the majority tradition.

The first minority tradition is that associated with the Anabaptists, the radical reformers of the sixteenth century. The term *Anabaptist* is used of many different groups in the sixteenth century. Some of them, such as the unitarian Socinians, have had no influence on Baptists. Others have definitely contributed certain ideas to modern Baptist life.

True Christians are a Sect Opposed to Society

The German scholar Ernst Troelsch once distinguished between two kinds of Christian groups, which he called the church-type and the sect-type.[52] By church-type he meant groups of Christians who are more or less at home in their society, who accept many things about their culture, and who contribute to and may even dominate the society and culture of which they are a part. They are inspired by the biblical passages which tell the people of Israel to inherit the promised land.

The sect-type are groups of Christians who are not at home in their society but are alienated from it. They resist their culture at almost every point. They make no effort to contribute to their society and culture or to dominate them, but only attempt to escape their influence as much as possible. They are inspired by the biblical passages which tell the church to love not the world or the things in the world.

Baptists began as a sect-type group. In the seventeenth century their ideas about baptism and about religious liberty were radical, and they were often persecuted for these. The Baptists in the American colonies continued to function as a sect-type group.

When Baptists accepted the revivalist emphasis on evangelism, things began to change. Baptists in America became a large group, and in a democratic nation, a large group is a powerful group. One recent book title expressed it vividly: *In the South the Baptists Are the Center of Gravity.*[53] They were transformed from a sect-type to a church-type in the South.

This does not mean that Southern Baptists accept everything about their society and culture. In many ways, they feel that their culture has become less Christian than it once was. Baptists have opposed things such as alcoholic beverages, casino gambling, and abortion. Nevertheless, they oppose these things, not as a tiny, insignificant minority, but as a large, influential group with good justification for thinking that they are entitled to influence society.

Among Southern Baptists in the twentieth century there are individuals who want Southern Baptists to return to the sect-type group they once were. They worry that the religion of Southern Baptists has become too much a religion of the nation, a "civil religion," rather than a personal, intentional commitment to follow Jesus Christ as his faithful disciples. For example, they are distressed by the fact that Southern Baptists conformed to Southern white society by accepting slavery in the nineteenth century and racial segregation in the twentieth, and they call Southern Baptists to return to a sect-type mentality which will enable them to resist the values of the larger society.

Southern Baptists have changed their attitudes toward race, but they did not become a sect-type group in order to do so. They began to change their attitude toward slavery when the South lost the Civil War, and they began to change their attitude toward segregation when the government of the United States made segregation illegal. Even now many Southern Baptist churches probably would not welcome black members with enthusiasm, which is ironic, given the deep commitment which Southern Baptists have toward missions. Stories circulate of black young people converted in Southern Baptist mission work abroad being denied membership in a local Southern Baptist congregation in the United States when they came here to attend college.

All is not gloomy, of course; many Baptist churches do welcome black members, and the Home Mission Board is working closely with predominantly black churches. Yet it cannot be said that the Southern Baptists have managed to oppose the segregationist values of Southern white society as successfully as a sect-type group might have done.

Christians Should Never Go to War

Across the centuries, Christians have held three different views about war. Some Christians believe in holy war; that is, they feel that God calls his people to go to war today as he called Israel long ago, and war is an activity which is God's will and is blessed by God. The most famous examples of Christians accepting holy war were the Crusades of the Middle Ages.

Many Christians hold a second view, called "just war theory." The idea is that war is an evil, not a good, but sometimes it is the lesser of two evils: not to go to war would be more evil than to go to war. Just war theory has two parts; certain criteria have been developed for determining when it is just to go to war (*jus ad bellum*), and other criteria have been developed for evaluation of whether a war is being conducted in a just manner (*jus in bello*). Examples of criteria for justly going to war include that the enemy has committed or threatened aggression, that every effort has been made to deal with the aggression short of war, that war has been officially declared, that there is a reasonable hope of victory, and that the gains of stopping the aggression will outweigh the suffering which the war will cause. Examples of criteria for conducting a war justly are that no actions be taken against noncombatants and that excessive force not be used. The majority of Christians have accepted the thesis of the just war theory that war is sometimes a regrettable necessity.

The third position toward war is that it is never the will of God for Christians to go to war or to use violence against others. The great inspiration for this view is, of course, the life and teachings of Jesus. He taught His followers not to return evil with evil, but to turn the other cheek. Many Christians, including many Anabaptists in the sixteenth century, therefore have chosen to be pacifists in order to be loyal to Christ.

Most Southern Baptists accept the just war theory. World War II is the example to which many refer when they talk about war. Was it not better, they ask, to resist Hitler and Naziism by means of war than to have abdicated our responsibility toward our European allies?

However, some Southern Baptists have called upon the Convention to adopt the pacifist position. A paper called *Baptist Peacemaker* and an organization called The Baptist Peace Fellowship of North America, while not exclusively pacifist, have led many Southern Baptists to think about this issue. The message of pacifism is attractive to Southern Baptists, not least because it appeals so directly to the teachings of Jesus, but the majority of Southern Baptists have not become pacifists.

Christians Should Share Their Possessions Communally

Christians have attempted various forms of communal life across the centuries, inspired by texts such as Acts 2:44-45:

> All the believers continued together in
> close fellowship and shared their belong-
> ings with one another. They would sell

their property and possessions, and dis-
tribute the money among all, according to
what each one needed.

The most famous examples of communal living are the
convents and monasteries found in the Eastern churches
and in the Roman Catholic Church, but other efforts at
communal living have been made. Some Anabaptists
practiced communal living, and in America in the nineteenth century numerous communities were formed
which held their possessions in common.

Most Southern Baptists have not been open to sugges-
tions that they share their possessions communally.
However, one influential Southern Baptist minister,
Clarence Jordan, did establish a successful experiment in
communal living, Koinonia Farm near Americus,
Georgia.

Like most Americans, many Southern Baptists have
heard the proposal that communal sharing of all things is
the only true form of justice. Two different understandings of justice operate in the public conversation in con-
temporary America. One view says that it is fair and just
for people to be able to benefit from what they have discovered, invented, earned, grown, or inherited; that it is
unjust to deprive them of what is theirs. The other view
says that it is fair and just for all Americans to have food,
clothing, housing, a good education, and meaningful
work.

The problem, of course, is that these two understandings of justice are incompatible. The only way to insure
that all Americans have food is to take away some of what
some people have earned and give it to those who either

cannot or do not successfully manage to earn enough to buy the food they need. It is not possible to have both of these kinds of justice in this world, for the securing of one of these forms of justice insures that the other will not be achieved.

The second understanding of justice receives great support from the prophets of Israel such as Amos, who often condemn the powerful people in Israel not only for stealing from the poor but for the fact that there are poor people in Israel at all. Most Americans feel the call to the first form of justice more deeply than the call to the second. In fact, the collapse of the governments of the Soviet Union and of Eastern Europe may suggest that people around the world feel the first form of justice more deeply than the second.

The second sense of justice gives rise to the formation of communes. The attractions of communal living are great, as witness the continuing success of religious orders in the Catholic Church, but among Southern Baptists, the call to communal sharing is decidedly a minority tradition.

The Anabaptists tradition still exercises an influence upon the Christian church generally and upon Southern Baptists in particular, especially in matters of peace and justice and the need to resist the values of the society and culture within which the church is obliged to live.

CHAPTER 6

Calvinistic Beliefs

The Baptists of the seventeenth and eighteenth centuries were very influenced by the theology of John Calvin and his followers. The great Baptist systematic theologian, John Gill, wrote as a Calvinist on almost every theological topic except baptism and church life. There were nuances in the Calvinism of the earliest Baptists, but they were revisions of Calvinism rather than rejections of it.

About a decade after the first Baptist church was formed in Holland, Dutch Calvinist church leaders met to resolve questions that had arisen concerning the exact meaning of Calvinism. In 1619 the Synod of Dort of the Dutch Reformed Church passed five articles which have become the norm for Calvinism. The five articles are often presented in English by the use of the acronym TULIP, which refers to total depravity, unconditional election, limited atonement, irresistible grace, and the final perseverance of the saints.[54]

All five of these distinctively Calvinistic beliefs are

related to salvation. Southern Baptists agree with Calvinists that salvation is a very important issue, and, as we have seen, they continue to believe in the final perseverance of the saints, as Calvinists do. This is the only one of the five themes from Dort which is part of the majority tradition of Southern Baptists.[55]

The other four themes are held by an articulate minority of Southern Baptists. Some of them teach in colleges and seminaries, and some have organized a group called The Founders Conference; the name reflects the fact that some of the founders of the Southern Baptist Convention such as James P. Boyce were devoted Calvinists. The Founders Conference publishes a journal called *The Founders Journal.*

Calvinism is an enormously attractive theological system. It has good claims to be true to Scripture, and it is conducive to personal humility, to corporate worship, and to sophisticated theological reflection. It is sometimes accused of being antithetical to evangelism and missions, and that is an understandable accusation; nevertheless, the Calvinists among Southern Baptists are very committed to missions and evangelism. Great evangelists such as George Whitefield and Jonathan Edwards were Calvinists; on the other hand, the great evangelist John Wesley moved away from Calvinism quite intentionally.

Our purpose here is to describe the major themes of Calvinism which are held by an articulate minority of Southern Baptists, and we shall follow the pattern given at the Synod of Dort.

All People are Totally Depraved

In Chapter 1 we noted that all Christians believe that the world is a fallen world and that all human beings are sinners. Calvinism takes that belief a step further. It says that all people are depraved.

The Bible can be called upon in support of this view. In Romans 7 Paul speaks of human beings as enslaved by sin, and in Ephesians 2 he speaks of people as dead in their sins; these texts certainly sound like descriptions of total depravity.

How are we to understand Paul's language of being enslaved to sin and being dead in sin? Calvinism understands these teachings to mean two things. First, human beings cannot save themselves; if they are to be saved, it must be by God. Second, until they have been born again, human beings are unable to respond to God; since they are spiritually dead, they cannot repent or have faith in God or pray.

All Christians, and all Southern Baptists, agree with the first interpretation. Human beings cannot save themselves. Human beings are dependent upon God for their salvation.

However, most Southern Baptists do not agree with the second interpretation. They think that the texts about being enslaved to sin and dead in sin mean that we are unable to save ourselves, but not that we are unable to turn to God with prayers of repentance and faith. "Whosoever will may come," Baptists sing, urging people to come to Christ for salvation.

Calvinists defend their belief that spiritually dead people cannot respond to God by saying that, if human beings were able to repent and have faith, they would be contributing to their salvation. But the majority of Southern Baptists do not agree. They believe that salvation is entirely a work of God done by his grace freely and generously given. Faith and repentance are responses made by persons who are still enslaved and dead in their sins, by which they receive salvation and new life which God has provided by his work in Jesus Christ. Repentance and faith do not contribute to salvation; they are the way one who is enslaved by sin receives the salvation from sin which God has provided.

God Unconditionally Elects some People to be Saved

The Bible has a great deal to say about election and predestination. Calvinists have studied this closely and have concluded that God has predestinated some individuals to be saved and others to be damned. The usual name for this view is "double predestination."[56]

This is not a view held by most Southern Baptists. They believe that God chooses to save those who choose to put their faith in Christ. Baptists are open to the idea that God has foreknowledge of which individuals will put their faith in Christ, but they do not believe that God in his sovereignty elects to save some and not others. They believe that God wants all to be saved but that he will not override their freedom in order to save them; if they make a decision to accept Christ, God saves them; if they make a decision to reject Christ, God sadly allows them to remain unsaved. There is nothing which God could have done to save them, which he has not done.

Most Southern Baptists are uneasy with the Calvinistic understanding of double predestination which seems to them to be arbitrary and cruel. They do not know how to reconcile it to their conviction that God "will have all men to be saved, and to come unto the knowledge of the truth" (1 Tim. 2:4). They are aware that some biblical texts sound very much like double predestination, such as "Jacob have I loved, but Esau have I hated" (Rom. 9:13), but they tend to read these texts in light of other texts such as "The Lord is not . . . willing that any should perish, but that all should come to repentance" (2 Peter 3:9).

Southern Baptists are uneasy with double predestination for another reason. As we have seen, they emphasize evangelism and missions. Their belief in evangelism and missions is supported by certain other beliefs. One of these is that God wants everyone to be saved, and a second one is that Christians can make it possible for people who otherwise could not be saved to be saved by preaching the gospel to them, that is, by evangelism and missions. Southern Baptists tend to resist beliefs which would undermine the enterprise of missions and evangelism, and many of them see double predestination as doing that. As was said earlier, it need not do so; there have been and are very evangelistic and missions-minded Calvinists. But since Southern Baptists are accustomed to the belief that it is God's will for everyone to be saved as a support for their missions and evangelism, they hold onto that support with the same determination with which they are committed to missions and evangelism.

Christ Died for the Elect Only

The New Testament presents the meaning of the death of Christ in many ways. For example, it is presented as a sacrifice which takes away sins, as a victory over the devil, as a revelation of the love of God, and as an example which Christians are to follow.[57]

All of these understandings of the death of Christ may be found in the writings of John Calvin. Along with them, Calvin presented an understanding of the atonement which became the most important one for many of his successors. Drawing upon Isaiah 53 and other biblical passages, he argued that when Christ died, he was acting as a substitute for sinners and experiencing God's punishment upon the sins of the world. The name for this understanding of the death of Christ is "penal substitution," "penal" because Christ was experiencing the penalty for sin and "substitution" because Christ was the substitute for sinners.

The penal substitutionary understanding of Christ's atoning work may be interpreted quantitatively. That is, it is quite reasonable to ask of this understanding, "Did Christ suffer the penalty for the sins of all people, or only the penalty for the people who are going to be saved?" The Calvinist answer is that Christ paid the penalty for the sins of the elect only, not for the sins of the entire world. This view is called "limited atonement" because it says that God intended the atonement to be for the sins of a limited group, the elect, and not for the sins of the entire world. The view that Christ died for the sins of all the world is called "general atonement."

Both views appeal to the New Testament. For example, Paul said that "Christ died for *our* sins,"(1 Cor. 15-3) which can be understood as a reference to a limited atonement. And John wrote that Christ "is the propitiation for our sins: and not for ours only, but also for the sins of the whole world" (1 John 2:2), which supports a general atonement.

In Calvinism, limited atonement is part of a tightly organized system of thought within which double predestination is very important. God elects some, but not all, to be saved; atonement is understood primarily as the bearing of a punishment, which can be quantified; therefore, Christ bore the penalty for the sins of the elect only. When people say that Christ bore the punishment for the sins of all people, even those who were not predestined to be saved, they are suggesting that some of his suffering, the part for the elect, was productive of a good result but that the other part of his suffering, the part for the nonelect, was, so to speak, wasted. Given their system of thought, it is understandable that Calvinists came to think that Christ died for the elect only.

The majority of Southern Baptists do not accept the system of theology within which limited atonement is a natural component, and their commitment to evangelism makes it important to them to be able to say to people who are not Christians, enthusiastically and with no subtle qualifications, "Christ died for your sins." Although penal substitution is not mentioned in *The Baptist Faith and Message*, many Southern Baptists are comfortable with it, but most are uncomfortable with the assertion that Christ intended to provide an atonement only for the elect.

God's Grace is Finally Irresistible

The last belief of Calvinists is closely tied to the earlier beliefs. It is that God's grace cannot finally be resisted by sinners. If God acts in grace to awaken sinners to faith and repentance, they will inevitably come to have faith and repentance and so to be saved.

Calvinists believe that God acts with a grace which in some mysterious way is finally irresistible; he does this toward some sinners, the elect, and not toward others, the non-elect. They believe that a theology which does not affirm the final irresistibility of God's grace effectively impugns the sovereignty of God. They ask, "If sinners—who are dead in their sins at that—can finally resist God, then who exactly is in charge of the world?"

Most Southern Baptists do not believe in the final irresistibility of God's grace. They believe that people can and do finally resist God's grace and that such resistance results in their never being saved.

Southern Baptists believe that God is very much in charge of the world, but that he has chosen to give human beings the power to make decisions which God will then respect. They believe that for God to give such freedom and then to respect it does not constitute a diminishment of the sovereignty of God but a recognition of the way in which the sovereign God has chosen to relate to his world.

In conclusion, what remains of the TULIP of Calvinism among the majority of Southern Baptists is the final belief, that all the saints persevere to the end. Total depravity, understood as the inability of unregenerate sinners to respond in faith to God, is rejected by the majority of Southern Baptists, along with belief in unconditional election, limited atonement, and the irresistibility of God's grace.

Theologians in early the Southern Baptist Convention

such as James P. Boyce and John L. Dagg were much more committed to the theological system of Calvinism than most Southern Baptists are today. In this sense, the minority of Southern Baptists who believe in Calvinism are right to point out that Southern Baptists have changed. This minority is entitled to think that they are conservatives attempting to retrieve a tradition which many Southern Baptists once held but have since lost.

But there is a complicating factor. Historian Walter Shurden has pointed out that when the Convention was organized in 1845, it already comprised four traditions.[58] The Convention included what Shurden called a Charleston tradition comprising the theological system of Calvinism. It also included a Sandy Creek tradition which minimized Calvinism and emphasized evangelism. It also included a Georgia tradition, which represented the Southernness and regionalness of the Convention, and a Tennessee tradition, which emphasized the distinctiveness of Baptist churches. To these four John Loftis has added a fifth, an evangelical-denominational tradition which is very strong in the Southwest.[59]

The point here is that among the founders of the Southern Baptist Convention there were men who were fully committed to Calvinism, but there were others for whom the center of gravity was not to be found here but rather in the commitment of the Convention to evangelism. To put it differently, evangelism, with its presuppositions and implications, was a commitment which was sufficient for the formation and operation of the Convention for some Baptists but not for others. Since the Convention was a hybrid from its inception, it is possible to speak of the widespread lack of commitment to some of the Calvinist beliefs today, not as a defection, but as the triumph of one of the early traditions over another. The Sandy Creek tradition has won out in the hearts of the majority of Southern Baptists over the Charleston tradition.

CHAPTER 7

Landmark Baptist Beliefs

The Landmark Baptist movement had its origin in the Northern United States early in the nineteenth century. In the South the great leaders of the Landmark movement were J. R. Graves, J. M. Pendleton, and A. C. Dayton. By the late nineteenth century they had managed to make Landmark Baptist concerns the most discussed issues in Southern Baptist life. Those issues were essentially issues of ecclesiology. The movement took its name from Proverbs 22:28: "Remove not the ancient landmark, which thy fathers have set." Graves himself did not feel that he was starting a new movement which needed a new name; rather, he believed that he was simply a strict, old-fashioned Baptist, setting up old Baptist landmarks that had been allowed to fall down. The summary of the Landmark concerns is presented as two themes.

Baptists Should Separate from Non-Baptists

We have seen that Baptists hold two distinctive ideas about baptism, that it should be by immersion, and that only believers should be baptized. The result is a believers church.

The Landmark Baptists took this idea a step further. They reasoned that, if the New Testament teaches that a believers church is the only genuine church, it follows that Methodist and Presbyterian churches are not really churches at all but religious societies.

The Landmark attitude toward a believers church is different from the attitude which Baptists originally had toward a believers church. The original attitude was that a believers church was a dream for which many people longed, and then, in the seventeenth century, it became a dream come true, a privilege to be enjoyed, and a blessing from God.

The Landmark Baptists saw it differently; a believers church was the creation of a people who had been faithful to God's Word when others were unfaithful; it was the achievement of real Bible-believers, with the help of God no doubt, but their achievement all the same. The Landmark attitude toward those such as Methodists and Presbyterians who did not have a believers church was not one of sadness that they were missing a blessing, but of hostility and opposition because they were not being true to the New Testament.

The Landmark Baptists were prepared to follow the argument where it led, and it led them to believe that Baptists should separate from non-Baptists because of the latter's unfaithfulness to the New Testament. So, for example, J. M. Pendleton wrote a tract entitled "Ought Baptists to invite pedobaptists to preach in their pulpits?" (a "pedobaptist" is one who baptizes babies). J. R. Graves published the tract under the title, "An Old Landmark Reset."

One of the arguments by which the Landmark Baptists defended their views was historical. They felt that there had always been a faithful group in the world. Their historians saw the history of dissent in the church—the Montanists, the Donatists, the Waldenses, the Anabaptists, and so on—as constituting an unbroken chain of believers churches across the centuries. Just as Roman Catholics believed in apostolic succession, the claim that there was in the Roman church an unbroken chain of ordinations of priests and consecrations of bishops reaching back to the apostle Peter, so the Landmark Baptists affirmed a "trail of blood," the claim that there was an unbroken chain of believers baptisms reaching back to the New Testament churches. In effect, the trail of blood meant that there was a succession of Baptist churches, though by other names, across the centuries. This view is not held by many historians today. It supported the Landmark polemic against non-Baptists, but the historical sources do not support it.[60]

It is clear that the Landmark Baptist belief that Baptists should separate from non-Baptists has influenced the Southern Baptist Convention, for the Convention almost never enters into cooperative arrangements with non-Baptist groups. When the ecumenical movement was born early in the century, Southern Baptists took the leadership in forming a new organization, the Baptist World Alliance, as an alternative to participation in organizations which include non-Baptists.

Nevertheless, most Southern Baptists have not accepted the Landmark invitation to separate completely from non-Baptists or to conduct a continual warfare with them. The Convention as an organization is famously unecumenical, but Baptist people are as open to fellowship with persons of other denominations as are the members of other denominations. Given their commitment to restricting "pulpit affiliation," as they called it, to Baptists, Pendleton and Graves would be astonished to learn that in recent years the Southern Baptist Convention has heard sermons and addresses by the Presbyterian D. James Kennedy, the Bible church pastor Chuck Swindoll, and the Orthodox Franky Schaeffer.

Local Baptist Congregations Should Keep Their Cooperation with Each Other to a Minimum

Since the Landmark Baptists claimed that Baptist churches are the only churches which are true to the New Testament, one would assume that they would want Baptist churches to work together very closely with each other. In fact, the opposite is true.

Here is how they arrived at their surprising belief that cooperation between congregations should be minimal. They believed that local congregations are the only institutions which are mentioned in the New Testament. They pointed out that the New Testament never mentions organizations such as associations, conventions, mission boards, or publication boards. They also pointed out that in the New Testament, the word *ekklesia* (church) is used to refer to a local congregation, and they insisted that it is never used to refer to all the congregations collectively; they used the phrase "kingdom of God" to refer to the churches collectively.

From the fact that local congregations are the only institutions mentioned in the New Testament, the Landmark Baptists drew the conclusion that the creation of other institutions is unbiblical. To be biblical, each Baptist congregation should cooperate as little as possible with other congregations, since such cooperation led to the formation of unbiblical entities.

While this may seem odd today when we are surrounded by large denominations, a case can be made for it. For example, it makes a certain kind of sense to say that the decision about whether or not a person is suitable to serve as a missionary ought to be made by that person's local congregation rather than by a mission board whose members do not really know the person well. Further, local congregations are able to avoid the bureaucracies which are always found in large denominational organizations.

In a sense, the Landmark movement held a high church view of local congregations. They felt that each congregation has a special, sanctified status because it replicates the institutions of the New Testament.

The Landmark Baptists saw two important implications in their principle of non-cooperation. One was that the denomination ought to have as few organizations as possible and keep them as small and powerless as possible. The other was that the Lord's Supper should be observed only in local congregations, and only members of the local congregation should participate in it.

Both of these ideas have influenced the Convention.

The leaders of the Convention had to struggle against the Landmark influence in order to form the great organizations such as the Sunday School Board. Today that struggle is over, and Southern Baptists are committed to the large organizations which make it possible for them to carry out ministries together which they could never carry out if the congregations acted independently.

As for the Lord's Supper, it is quite easy to see the influence of the Landmark Baptists upon the Southern Baptist Convention. The Convention was organized at a meeting held at the First Baptist Church of Augusta, Georgia, in 1845, a few years before the Landmark influence became so pronounced. When the messengers to that meeting gathered, they took the Lord's Supper together. Today it is unthinkable that the messengers to a meeting of the Convention would take the Lord's Supper together.

With few exceptions, observances of the Lord's Supper in Southern Baptist life occur in local congregations. Most Baptists accept the Landmark interpretation that Jesus entrusted the ordinances, baptism and the Lord's Supper, to the churches rather than to an elite of ordained clergy. However, most Southern Baptist churches do not accept the strict Landmark view that only members of the local congregation can take the Lord's Supper. Some Southern Baptist churches follow that practice, but many others offer the Lord's Supper to all baptized believers, and still others offer it to all Christians of whatever denomination.

Graves claimed that he was attempting to get Baptists to return to their heritage; it is not a claim which historians today find plausible. There is considerable evidence that when Baptist churches were founded in the early seventeenth century, they made a great effort to express how much they had in common with other Christian churches. This was one of their purposes for adopting confessions. Leon McBeth points out:

> Baptists often used confessions not to
> proclaim "Baptist distinctives" but instead
> to show how similar Baptists were to
> other orthodox Christians.[61]

The early Baptists also were very committed to the little Baptist congregations working together very closely with each other, and they did not restrict participation in the Lord's Supper to members of the local congregation. Further, many interpreters today think that in Ephesians and elsewhere in the New Testament, the word *ekklesia* is used to refer to all the churches collectively, and almost no interpreter today accepts the Landmark understanding of the phrase "kingdom of God."

The Landmark Baptists set up some landmarks, but they were new ones, not old ones.

CHAPTER 8

Deeper Life Beliefs

All serious Christians are interested in Christian living, and thoughtful Christian leaders attempt to provide guidance and encouragement for all who want to live as faithful Christians. Across the centuries, the church has welcomed many varied insights concerning Christian living. With rare exceptions, no proposals concerning Christian living have been officially rejected by the church. The result of this openness is that quite diverse understandings of Christian living are to be found in the church across the centuries. The deeper life understanding is one of those.

In the middle of the nineteenth century, a distinctive understanding of Christian living developed in the United States and Great Britain. It is usually called the holiness movement although many insiders prefer to call it by the name of a very important early book which taught it, *The Higher Christian Life*. The book was published in 1859 and was written by W. E. Boardman, a Presbyterian minister.[62] Other proponents of this particular understanding of Christian living were Hannah Whitall Smith and Robert Pearsall Smith. They taught that there is a second experience, distinct from conversion, by which a Christian may arrive at a state of holiness. In England the movement became known as the Keswick Movement because an important conference was held annually at Keswick in the Lake District. Antecedents for the holiness movement are found in the Methodist concern for personal holiness and in the work of the evangelist Charles G. Finney.

The holiness movement of the nineteenth century gave birth to two new movements in the twentieth century. One is the Pentecostal movement, which began in Los Angeles early in the twentieth century under the leadership of a black holiness preacher, William J. Seymour. Pentecostals hold the holiness teaching about a second experience, distinct from conversion, and add to it the idea that speaking in tongues is a sign that one has had this experience. They call this experience "the baptism in the Holy Spirit."

For half a century the Pentecostal movement existed in America in two kinds of churches. One was the older holiness churches which accepted Pentecostalism, such as the Church of God (Cleveland, Tennessee); however, some holiness churches, such as the Church of God (Anderson, Indiana) and the Church of the Nazarene, resisted Pentecostalism. The second place where the Pentecostal movement existed was in newly formed Pentecostal denominations such as the Assemblies of God.

The second movement derived from the holiness movement is the deeper life movement. It is very similar to the holiness movement, except for two things. First, unlike the original movement, this movement does not always emphasize that the second experience be entirely distinct from the first. Second, in the deeper life movement the result of the second experience is not personal holiness; it speaks instead of a deeper life or a victorious life. The victorious life includes personal holiness but also includes other things such as inner peace, happiness, power in prayer, and success in one's work.

The deeper life movement is similar to Pentecostalism. The major difference between them is that Pentecostalism understands speaking in tongues to be the dispensable sign that one has received the baptism in the Spirit, and the deeper life does not.

None of those committed to the deeper life has felt any reason to leave the Convention. Some who speak in tongues remain within the Southern Baptist Convention, but others have left the Convention altogether, because the Convention has not been open to persons who speak in tongues.

Some of the leaders of the deeper life movement among Southern Baptists have been Peter Lord, Jack Taylor, and the late Bertha Smith and Jamie Buckingham. The movement is a loose network of persons and organizations, and it includes an attractive publication entitled *Fulness*.

Jack Taylor was formerly a pastor in Texas, and he is now a popular Bible teacher and conference leader. His understanding of the deeper Christian life is representative of the form in which this minority understanding has been presented to Southern Baptists. This understanding may be presented as four themes which are closely tied to each other.

Many Christians Do Not Know the Secret
of the Deeper Christian Life

The deeper life movement teaches that there is a secret to living as a faithful Christian. This secret is unknown not only to non-Christians and to less than fully committed Christians, but unknown even to very committed, serious Christians. Serious Christians who attempt to live as faithful disciples will fail because they do not know the secret of Christian living.

Jack Taylor expresses this in a personal story. He says that he has been through three stages in his life as a Christian. First, he thought it was easy to be a good Christian, and he threw himself into it. But he failed and became discouraged, and then he made a discovery which moved him into a second stage: he discovered that it is very difficult to be a good Christian. Once again he threw himself into trying to live as a good Christian, and once again he failed. Then he made a discovery which moved him into the third stage: he discovered that it is impossible to be a good Christian. Only with this discovery did he find the secret of a victorious Christian life.[63]

The Secret Is that Christians Must Not Strive,
But Depend upon God, to Live the Christian Life

Proponents of the deeper life recognize that many Christians do not seriously attempt to live as faithful Christians. This is an idea with which most observers would agree. The doctrine of the deeper life goes beyond this. It teaches that it is a mistake for committed Christians to attempt to live as faithful disciples.

Christians do not have within themselves the power to live faithfully. The only power that is adequate for the impossible task of Christian living, is the power of God. The attempt to live faithfully indicates that one is depending on one's own power rather than depending upon the power of God.

The secret of victorious living, then, is to cease striving. It is to become passive, so that God can give one the power to live faithfully. Hannah Whitall Smith, author of the very popular *The Christian's Secret of a Happy Life* (1875), once wrote: "In order for a lump of clay to be made into a beautiful vessel, it must be entirely abandoned to the potter, and must lie passive in his hands."[64] Passive dependence upon God is the only way to successful Christian living, and activity is a barrier to it.

When Christians Cease Striving and Depend upon God, God Will Work Through Them

Once Christians have discovered the secret of Christian victory, they then surrender their lives to God and depend totally upon him. This opens the way for God to work through them and to do through them what they could never have done on their own.

The deeper life movement speaks of the power of God in more or less the same terms that Christians have always used. It speaks of the power of the Spirit in one's life. It employs mystical phrases from the New Testament such as "Christ in you." In many ways, assurance is given that God will take control of the life of dependent Christians and do wonderful things through them.

Christians Who Do Not Strive but Depend upon God, Will Live Victoriously

The results of depending upon God are described in many ways. In the original holiness movement, the emphasis fell upon personal holiness or sanctification, that is, upon deliverance from personal sin and, in some cases, even from temptation. In the modern deeper life movement, a toned-down version of this idea is retained, and other emphases are added. Jack Taylor says of the key (the secret) to victorious living: "I have seen the key open the lock of personal disillusionment, marital disharmony, self condemnation, fear, anxiety, depression, and fling open the door upon a new and wonderful life!"[65]

The deeper life understanding of Christian living has a great goal and a great truth, and provides a great help. Its great goal is for Christians to experience God in their lives in ways that transform them. While some theologians minimize the experiential aspect of Christian faith, most Christians and many theologians believe that it is important to experience Christ's presence. The deeper life commitment to experiential religion is valuable.

The great truth which underlies the deeper life understanding of Christian living is that Christians are dependent on God. Christians sometimes forget their dependence upon God and begin to feel that they are quite independent; this feeling is very close to pride, and it is not realistic or morally appropriate. The greatest saints in all ages have emphasized their need of God's help at every moment of their lives.

The great help which the deeper life understanding has provided for people is a resolution of the frustration which Christians often feel when they have sincerely and conscientiously attempted to live faithfully and have failed. It is an experience which apparently the apostle Paul knew, for he wrote: "I don't do the good I want to do; instead, I do the evil that I do not want to do" (Rom. 7:19).

How are we to account for this experience? The deeper life has a simple answer: You tried to live faithfully and you failed, because you tried in your own strength; if you will stop trying and depend completely upon God, then God will do through you what you clearly are unable to do for yourself.

This deeper life understanding has been an enormous help to many Christians and that it will continue to help many in the future. Its goal of experiential religion is altogether admirable, and its emphasis upon our dependence upon God is always to be welcomed by serious Christians.

Nevertheless, four things should be noticed. First, the New Testament does not teach that there is a secret to Christian living. In fact, the idea that there is a secret to Christian living is incompatible with the openness with which the understanding of the entire experience of salvation is presented by the New Testament writers. The New Testament churches resisted gnosticism in part because of its claims to have a secret, arcane knowledge available only to an initiated elite.

Second, Christian living is not only a matter of passivity but also of activity. The New Testament everywhere calls upon Christians to live obedient lives; all of this is written on the assumption that intentional obedience is possible and is a good thing. A popular hymn speaks of

God's call to all Christians to "Trust and Obey." This is a more balanced presentation than the deeper life message, "Depend, Don't Strive."

Third, God does not begin to provide his power only when Christians cease striving and begin to be totally passive and dependent. Instead, the New Testament teaches that God is always providing his power to help all his people. God gives them the Gospel, which is the power of God unto salvation (Rom. 1:16). He gives them the church, which is the body of Christ through which Jesus mediates his power to his people. The texts about "Christ in you (Col. 1:27) speak of a reality which is enjoyed not by a spiritual elite who know and practice a secret which other Christians do not know, but by all Christians by virtue of their faith in Christ. God gives all Christians his Word, which is powerful (Heb. 4:12); it is not necessary for one to discover a secret in order to experience the power of God's Word, but only to believe and attempt to obey the Word. God gives powerful spiritual gifts to all his people (1 Cor. 12:3), not just to a small group who know the secret of Christian living. In short, it is a mistake to say that God works powerfully only in the lives of those who know a secret of depending upon God; the New Testament teaches that God works powerfully in the lives of all his people, all the time. Christians are to cooperate with God; that cooperation includes depending on God, but it also includes attempting to be obedient to God.

Fourth, the deeper life movement no longer uses the explicit language of moral perfection, but underneath the language which the movement uses lies an implicit promise of perfection upon earth. By constantly talking about the deeper life, the higher life, the overcoming life, the victorious life, the happy life, and the fulness of life, the movement suggests the possibility of perfection.[66] The understanding of the church in the New Testament era and across the centuries is that perfection is a promise which Christians may look forward to in the life to come and a standard toward which they are to strive in the present life, but it is not a state at which they can arrive in this life. As Paul wrote, "I do not claim that I have already succeeded or have already become perfect. I keep striving to win the prize for which Christ Jesus has already won me to himself" (Phi. 3:12).

The appeal of the deeper life among Southern Baptists has been very great. A vocal and influential minority of Southern Baptists has accepted all four beliefs: that there is a secret to Christian living, that the secret is to stop striving and begin depending on God, that God works powerfully through those who do this, and that those who do it live victorious lives.

CHAPTER 9

Fundamentalist Beliefs

Throughout most of the nineteenth century, the various Protestant denominations spent a lot of time and energy arguing against each other; we have seen how Landmark Baptists did this vigorously. But a new theology arose in the nineteenth century, the product of the Enlightenment; it was called "liberal Protestantism." As it became stronger in the United States in the late nineteenth century, it began to pose a serious threat to conservative Christians in all the Protestant denominations. This led some of them to set aside their denominational differences in order to form a loose coalition to act as a united front against the common enemy, liberalism. Curtis Lee Laws, a newspaper editor, coined the term "fundamentalist" to describe his fellow Baptists who were defending the faith against liberalism, and the word soon came to be used for the loose coalition of conservatives from many denominations which was formed to fight liberalism.

Fundamentalism quickly became a threat to many Protestants and others, and they reacted to it. Some, such as Harry Emerson Fosdick, urged the churches to resist fundamentalism; Fosdick preached a famous sermon to this effect, entitled "Shall the Fundamentalists Win?" Others, such as the journalist H. L. Mencken, spoke contemptuously of fundamentalists as "Neanderthals."

The contempt of Mencken and others has stuck; the word *fundamentalist* still carries connotations of contempt. The term *fundamentalist* will be used here only for those persons who lived earlier in the century and who referred to themselves as fundamentalists. What will be pointed out is that some people today hold some of the same views that people such as Curtis Lee Laws held. This is done only in order to understand the views better, not to express contempt for them.

A conventional interpretation of fundamentalism is that it is the religion of a marginal group of rural, uneducated, Southern Protestants. This proposal is interesting because it is wrong on every count. Fundamentalism was much stronger in the North than in the South, much stronger in cities than in the countryside, and many of its leaders, at least in its early period, were intellectuals such as J. Gresham Machen.[67]

Several scholars have studied fundamentalism carefully and have helped us understand it more accurately. They have offered several interpretations of the theology of fundamentalism. Ernest Sandeen proposed that fundamentalism was formed by the merger of two previously separate theological traditions.[68] The first was a tradition which affirmed the inerrancy of the original manuscripts of the Bible, proposed by theologians such as Charles Hodge and B. B. Warfield at Princeton Theological Seminary. The other was a tradition of dispensationalism and premillennialism associated with Bible schools such as Moody Bible Institute.

What is interesting about this proposal is that, prior to the formation of the fundamentalist coalition, these two groups had opposed each other vigorously. The Princeton theologians were emphatically not premillennialists, and the Bible school leaders tended to emphasize the King James Version of the Bible rather than the original manuscripts. Nevertheless, the two groups joined forces in order to resist the common enemy, liberalism.

More recently, George Marsden has proposed that two other theological strands were also part of the formation of fundamentalism. One was revivalism and the other was the deeper life movement; both were closely associated with the great evangelist D. L. Moody. Marsden is right: It is important to recognize that fundamentalism emphasizes conversion and evangelism as much as it does its other beliefs.[69]

In order to understand fundamentalism, it is also necessary to remember what brought together people who earlier had been divided along these lines as well as along denominational lines. It was their determination to resist liberalism. They did not organize just to create a fellowship without liberals; they organized to create a common front for the battle against liberalism.

We may, therefore, think of fundamentalism as the bringing together of four separate theological traditions and of a new component. The new component is militant resistance to theological liberalism, and the four traditions are revivalism, the deeper life understanding of Christian living, the inerrancy of the autographs of the Bible, and premillennialism.

There are three remaining themes of fundamentalism.

True Christians Should Oppose Liberalism Militantly

George Dollar is a historian who has taught at Bob Jones University, which is in some ways the flagship institution of fundamentalism. He is the author of a large and authoritative history of fundamentalism. In it he defines fundamentalism as follows: "Historical Fundamentalism is the literal exposition of all the affirmations and attitudes of the Bible and the militant exposure of all non-Biblical affirmations and attitudes."[70]

The word "militant" is important. Dollar believes that a fundamentalist must not only believe what the Bible teaches, and oppose the teachings contrary to the Bible, but also be militant in opposing teachings contrary to the Bible. From the point of view of a fundamentalist, it is morally wrong to believe the Bible and then fail to be militant in one's opposition to unbiblical teachings. A text much loved by fundamentalists is: "Earnestly contend for the faith which was once delivered unto the saints" (Jude 3, KJV).

In this sense, most Southern Baptists did not become fundamentalists. It is true that some Southern Baptist leaders contributed to the collection of booklets called *The Fundamentals*, one of the defining documents of the fundamentalist movement. It also is true that Southern Baptists are a conservative Protestant group. But in the 1920s and 1930s, the Southern Baptists rejected a policy of militancy in their opposition to liberal teachings.

One famous Southern Baptist pastor attempted to lead Southern Baptists to become militant in their opposition to liberalism. His name was J. Frank Norris, and he was the pastor of the First Baptist Church of Fort Worth,

Texas. Many Southern Baptists believed his message that some of the schools of the Convention were becoming liberal, and many worried about it. In fact, some limited actions were taken concerning alleged liberalism among Southern Baptists. But the overall decision of the Convention was to follow not Norris's leadership but that of George W. Truett, the pastor of the First Baptist Church of Dallas. Norris's church was expelled from the Baptist General Convention of Texas in 1924; Truett was elected president of the Southern Baptist Convention in 1927.

The logic of fundamentalism is very persuasive. It says that, since God gives us his truth, we ought not only to believe it and to teach it but to fight for it. What could be wrong with that?

The answer, of course, is that militancy toward other Christians destroys Christian community. Once the fighting begins, people become suspicious of one another and angry at one another. Militancy destroys cooperation and fellowship. This is especially serious for Southern Baptists, many of whom do not have an understanding of the universal church or of Christian unity to hold them together. Cooperation, trust, and fellowship are the only ties which bind them to one another, and if these fail, the Convention has nothing to fall back on to keep it together.

The Original Manuscripts of the Bible Were Inerrant

Chapter 1 showed that Christians across the centuries have agreed that the Bible is the uniquely inspired Word of God and that it is authoritative for the faith and life of Christians. Christians have used the words "infallible" (unfailing) and "inerrant" (unerring) to describe this understanding of the Bible. Chapter 2 explains that Protestants assert the principle that the Bible alone is the Word of God.

In the nineteenth century some liberal Protestant scholars came to the conclusion that the Bible contains errors. Naturally, conservative scholars set out to refute this view, and some of them adopted a new strategy for doing so. They acknowledged that some errors may exist in the texts and translations of the Bible which we have today, including the King James Version, but they argued that these errors came into modern texts and translations during the process of transmission of the Bible; the original Hebrew and Greek manuscripts, they said, were without errors of any kind.

Many Christians are not familiar with the fascinating story of the transmission of the Bible. The oldest parts of the Bible were written more than a thousand years before Christ, and the latest parts several decades after Christ. For about fourteen hundred years, all copies of the Bible were handwritten. Printing by movable type was not invented in Europe until the middle of the fifteenth century; Johannes Gutenberg, the inventor of the new process of printing, published his great Bible in 1460. Naturally, many of the handwritten copies contain slight variations. Biblical scholars are very skilled at retrieving what the writers of the Bible originally wrote, so much so that we may have very great confidence in the texts which we have today, but many variations do occur in the texts which were copied by hand before the invention of printing.

In the nineteenth century, scholars at Princeton Theological Seminary and elsewhere began to argue that, even though modern texts and translations of the Bible might contain errors, the original manuscripts of the Bible did not contain any errors, not even small errors concerning trivial matters. The leaders of the fundamentalist movement accepted this procedure of defending the truth of the Bible by appealing to the original manuscripts. The original manuscripts are called the "autographs," which means "the writings themselves," and everyone agrees that they were all lost centuries ago; they do not exist today. That is why I used the past tense in stating this theme: "The original manuscripts of the Bible were inerrant."

The Princeton theology also put a new twist on the traditional Christian conviction that the Bible is God's truthful Word. It extended the truthfulness of the Bible to factors such as science and history as well as faith and morals; it affirmed the truthfulness of the details of the Bible as well as of its general message. However, as we have seen, it restricted that truthfulness to the original manuscripts, and it concluded that the texts and translations which we have today are true only to the extent that these accurately present what was written in the original manuscripts.

As is well known, biblical inerrancy in this technical sense was much debated in the 1970s and 1980s. Many books were written to defend the idea and others to refute it, and an International Council on Biblical Inerrancy was formed to defend it. The Council issued three famous statements about the Bible, one of which has become a benchmark of the meaning of biblical inerrancy today; it is called "The Chicago Statement on Biblical Inerrancy."[71] It is a very sophisticated, nuanced statement, and many scholars feel that it offers the best model for affirming the Bible in our time.

Some Southern Baptists scholars accept the modern, technical understanding of biblical inerrancy presented in "The Chicago Statement," and others do not.[72] Since 1979, those who have accepted this idea have been assuming leadership in the Convention, and one result is that the idea is now more widely known and discussed than it was before. A very sophisticated and winsome presentation of that view was disseminated among Southern Baptists as an annual doctrinal study book in 1992.[73]

As might be expected, the new technical vocabulary of inerrancy of the autographs is not found in *The Baptist Faith and Message* (I). That document affirms that the Bible has "God for its author, salvation for its end, and truth without any mixture of error for its matter."

Two things should be noted about this statement. First, *The Baptist Faith and Message* nowhere refers to the original manuscripts of the Bible, so it is natural to infer that the document is referring to the texts and translations of the Bible available to us today.

Second, the phrase "for its matter" is ambiguous; it may refer to every detail recorded in the Bible, or it may refer to the great message of the Bible. *The Baptist Faith and Message* nowhere refers to matters of science and history, and a sentence in the preface says that "the sole authority for faith and practice among Baptists is the Scriptures of the Old and New Testaments." It is plausible, therefore, to interpret the phrase "its matter" to refer to issues of "faith and practice."

Christ Will Return to Earth and Rule for a Thousand Years

Chapter 1 showed that hope is an indispensable component of the Christian tradition and that it is shared by all Christians. Christians have always had hope for both the present world and the world to come. The customary word for referring to the Christian hope for the world to come is "heaven," and the customary phrase for referring to the Christian hope for the present world is "the kingdom of God."

In the nineteenth century, many Christians began to employ another word for their hope for the present world, the word "millennium," which means "thousand years." The word does not occur in the Bible, but there are several references to a thousand-year rule of Christ in Revelation 20:1-9. During the nineteenth century some biblical scholars, especially in Britain and the United States, emphasized the millennium in their teaching, and people in many churches came to feel that the millennium is the best way to express the Christian hope concerning this world and the end of this world. That view was dominant in the fundamentalist movement.

There are three general understandings of the millennium. One is that the thousand years referred to in Revelation 20 is a symbol, perhaps for the church or for heaven. This view is supported by the fact that the book of Revelation contains many symbols. This view is called amillennialism, which means *no millennium*, because it does not interpret Revelation 20 to refer to a literal thousand-year reign of Christ upon earth.

The second view is postmillennialism. It was the dominant view in many churches in the nineteenth century. It presents the millennium as a reign of Christ upon earth; however, it sees that reign as spiritual rather than literal. Postmillennialism teaches that the Spirit will guide and empower the church to do its work in the world so that more and more of the world will come to have faith in Christ, and Christ's reign will be extended over most of the people on earth; the result will be an era of peace and progress, of faith and brotherhood. That era is the millennium, and it will be completed by Christ returning in person to the earth and accepting the homage which almost all the world will then wish to give him.

Postmillennialism is a very optimistic view, and it empowered much of the great missionary movement of the nineteenth century. It received its most serious setback with the global traumas of the twentieth century. The World Wars, the great depression, and other expressions of evil in the world, make it difficult to believe that the world is making progress in the way postmillennialists had thought.

The third view is called premillennialism, and it has become very popular in the twentieth century. It is quite pessimistic about the possibility of progress in the world. It pictures the world as getting worse and worse, and even the church as becoming less and less faithful to Christ; this will continue until the moment when Christ suddenly returns and establishes his kingdom on earth.

There are two types of premillennialism. The historic type, held by many Christians across the centuries, is that Christ will return suddenly and establish his rule for a thousand years; he will then judge the world, and history will come to an end.

In the nineteenth century, certain biblical scholars developed a much more elaborate understanding of premillennialism. It is called dispensational premillennialism, and it is well represented by a study Bible which was written by C. I. Scofield early in the twentieth century. Scofield taught that God has related to human beings differently in different ages, or dispensations; he located seven dispensations in the Bible. The first was innocence, which ended when Adam and Eve were banished from the Garden of Eden. The second was conscience, which ended with the Great Flood. The third was human government, which ended with the Tower of Babel. The fourth was promise, which ended with the captivity of Israel in Egypt. The fifth was law, which ended when Christ died. The sixth is grace, and it is in place now and will continue until the final judgment. The seventh is the kingdom of God, which is yet to come.

Dispensationalism is the background against which Scofield and others developed their understanding of the end of the world. They attempted to piece together what is said about the future of the world in various texts of the Old and New Testaments, and they came out with a sequence as follows. First, the world will continue to degenerate. Then, when no one expects it (though there are signs which point to it), Christ will come in the sky (not to the earth) and gather up all Christians, living and dead, to be with Him; this is called the rapture of the church. Then, for seven years, the earth will experience the most awful suffering in history; this is called the great tribulation. Next, Christ will return to earth with his church and will establish himself as the ruler of the world, and will bind Satan. Christ will rule the earth for a thousand years; this is the millennium. Then, Satan will be released and will gather his people together, and Christ will gather all his people together, and they will fight a great battle; this is called Armageddon. Christ will defeat his enemies. Finally, the world will be judged, and all people will go either to heaven or to hell for eternity.

Dispensational premillennialism has become very popular with Southern Baptists in the twentieth century, and many are surprised to learn that premillennialism has not always been the dominant view among Baptists. Baptist confessions of faith are quite neutral about the details of the end of the world. *The Baptist Faith and Message* (X) says quite noncommittally,

> God, in his own time and in his own way,
> will bring the world to its appropriate
> end. According to his promise, Jesus
> Christ will return personally and visibly in
> glory to the earth.

As one popular phrase has it, when it comes to the return of Christ, it is best to serve on the welcoming committee and to avoid the planning committee.

These, then, are three themes, closely associated with the fundamentalist coalition which was formed in the United States early in the twentieth century, which have been offered as a minority view to Southern Baptists: militant opposition to liberalism, inerrancy of the non-extant, original, Hebrew and Greek manuscripts of the Bible, and dispensational premillennialism.

CHAPTER 10

Progressive Beliefs

The five sets of proposed alternative beliefs examined so far come from the right side of the Convention. That is, they claim, with more or less justification, to be traditional Baptist beliefs which should receive more emphasis in the life of the Convention.

The beliefs to be reviewed in the present chapter come from the left rather than the right. That is, they are not presented as part of the Baptist tradition which has been forfeited, but are acknowledged by their sponsors to be new proposals which are appropriate for the life of the Southern Baptists in the future.

Unlike the earlier five sets of proposed alternatives, those in this chapter are not closely tied to each other. The only thing they have in common is that they are not traditional. What this means, in practical terms, is that some Southern Baptists will hold to some of these beliefs and reject some of the others. The customary term used of these beliefs by those who reject them is *liberal.* I have avoided that term because the beliefs are not all associated with liberal Protestantism, and because, in the United States today, in both political and religious discourse, the term is usually pejorative.

The beliefs to be described here are not the only progressive proposals which have been made to Southern Baptists. They are the most important progressive proposals, and they are representative of the others. Because these beliefs are unrelated to each other, the sequence in which they are presented is of no importance.

Women Should Be Ordained and Serve as Pastors

The story of the place of women in the life of the Southern Baptists has been told by H. Leon McBeth and others.[74] It is a story whose outline is similar to that of the place of women in American public life generally. Early in the life of the Southern Baptists, women were excluded from being messengers to the Convention.[75] Women did not serve as pastors of churches. Nevertheless, they were active in many areas of Southern Baptist life. They bore much of the burden of ministry in many local churches. They were missionaries, and they organized societies for securing support for missions in the United States and abroad. They were church musicians and teachers of children and youth.

Women first attended the Convention as messengers in 1877. Prior to that time, they had formed the Woman's Missionary Union, an organization of their own devoted to missions education and support which met simultaneously with the Convention. In 1905, the first woman addressed the Convention. Women were allowed to vote in the Convention beginning in 1918, two years before women were allowed to vote in American political elections. The first woman chosen as an officer of the Convention was Marie Mathis, who was elected second vice-president in 1963.[76]

In many small steps, women have become more involved in the life of the Convention and more influential in the Convention. The big step, the most difficult step, concerned ordination to serve as a pastor. That step seems to have been taken first in 1964.[77]

Ordination is conducted among Southern Baptists by local congregations, not by associations or conventions. This means that each local congregation can decide for itself whether or not to ordain a woman. Most have not ordained women and would not do so under any circumstances, but some have. The number of ordained Southern Baptist women is now several hundred. Many of these serve as military chaplains for whom ordination is required. All Southern Baptist military chaplains are endorsed by the Home Mission Board.

Very few women serve as pastors of churches. Those who oppose an expanded role for women in the Convention have drawn a line at the point of ordaining women to serve as pastors. Here is an eloquent expression of opposition to the ordination of women pastors:

> Ordination says to the world that the church is placing the highest authority of the ordaining church in the hands of the person being ordained. Since Scripture states that "I do not permit a woman to teach or to have authority over a man" (1 Timothy 2:11), the ruling pastor-teacher

> should be a man. The pastor-teacher
> should be in complete authority over the
> public worship service. At his discretion a
> woman may be called on to pray, to give
> testimony, but it should be done with
> respect to the pastor's position, not to take
> over the service.[78]

Those who favor the ordination of women to serve as pastors see no reason to draw any lines about how women may serve in the churches. They understand the New Testament passages such as the one which Mrs. Kaemmerling quoted to have been God's will in the setting of the first century, when a woman's exercise of authority over men would have created a scandal and so hindered the work of the Gospel. However, they feel that in the setting of the modern world, where women routinely exercise authority over men in business, government, and the professions, it creates a scandal and hinders the work of the gospel to exclude them from a similar role in the church.

There is another issue here also, the issue of authority. Objections to the ordination of women are often premised on the idea that ordination confers authority. But does it?

There are three basic understandings of the theological meaning of ordination in the church.[79] The Roman Catholic understanding is that ordination confers an indelible grace which authorizes a man to offer the Mass. The magisterial Reformation understanding is that ordination confers the authority to preach the Gospel. The third understanding rejects both of the others, defining ordination as the giving of a communal blessing to a person who feels called to service and is willing to follow that call.

This third understanding is much more compatible with the Baptist theological heritage than the others. Nevertheless, those who have resisted the ordination of women to serve as pastors have spoken repeatedly of the second view.

The Bible Should Be Studied Critically

The story of the rise of biblical criticism in the nineteenth century has been told many times. The Southern Baptists, like many other Christian groups, initially resisted much of the critical study of the Bible. Eventually many Southern Baptists came to accept textual criticism, the attempt to determine the best Hebrew and Greek texts of the Bible. However, other forms of criticism, such as source criticism, form criticism, and redaction criticism, are still resisted by many Southern Baptists.

A minority of Southern Baptists has proposed that all responsible criticism be accepted. The argument in support of biblical criticism is that the Bible is a human as well as a divine book, and that the human dimension means that the Bible and should be studied in the same way any other book from the ancient world is studied. Further, the argument is that the critical study of the Bible is a helpful way to understand the message of the Bible, which is the goal of all Bible study. Some have also argued that critical Bible study serves a conservative function, acting as a restraint on bizarre interpretations of the Bible.

Many Southern Baptists, like many people in other denominations, do not know what biblical criticism is. When they hear the phrase "criticism of the Bible," they ask, "Why would any Christian want to criticize the Bible?" The phrase is an unhappy one, and this led one great Southern Baptist teacher, C. Penrose St. Amant, to propose that the phrase "biblical criticism" be replaced with "biblical analysis."[80]

When does Bible study become critical? Perhaps the most helpful answer is that the study of any text becomes critical when one no longer simply learns from the text but begins to generate questions of one's own and to put them to the text.[81] This definition helps us to recognize that even though many Christians oppose biblical criticism, many of them have benefited from it, and not only at the level of textual criticism. For example, conservative teachers are as likely as more progressive ones to begin their teaching about a book of the Bible with information about its author, date, and purpose. These are our questions, not those of the biblical writers, and the study by which we attempt to answer them is critical in the sense indicated, a fact often unacknowledged by those who continue to think of themselves as opposed to biblical criticism. Conservative scholars distinguish carefully between a "believing criticism," and the historical-critical method. They believe the historical-critical method to be incompatible with faith in the truthfulness of the Bible and not value-neutral.

Two things remain to be said. One is that the resistance to biblical criticism often is a resistance to particular conclusions which have been reached by particular biblical critics. For example, for a very long time many biblical critics believed that John's Gospel was produced by a Gentile with no appreciation for the Jewishness of Jesus and His message. This view disturbed those who felt that the Gospel was, as it claimed to be, apostolic. As it turns out, the critics were wrong, and the Jewishness of the fourth Gospel is now accepted by biblical scholars.[82]

The other thing to be said is that fewer and fewer scholars are prepared to defend the idea that biblical criticism is the only form of Bible study. Criticism is a relatively modern development, and many scholars are now at work retrieving the kinds of Bible study which the church did before criticism achieved its dominance. In fact, one very learned theologian at Oxford University, Andrew Louth, has even made a case for the usefulness of the allegorical study of the Bible.[83] While this is an extreme view, what is clear is that many Bible scholars are now open to the idea that criticism must take its place as one of several methods of Bible study.

Among Southern Baptists, however, it remains true that those who propose that critical study of the Bible be done, remain a progressive minority.

The Best Higher Education is Exploration Not Indoctrination

For purposes of analysis, higher education, including theological education, is to be thought of as a range with four options. The options, moving from right to left, are brainwashing, indoctrination, exploration, and relativization.

Brainwashing is a coercive form of education which overwhelms students and force-feeds them with information that they are in no position to resist. No one in Southern Baptist life believes in brainwashing.

Indoctrination is not coercive. It understands the primary purpose of education to be the faithful transmission of a heritage by teachers to students. This transmission includes active resistance to views that contest the heritage. If the teacher refers to views that contest the heritage, it is only to refute them and to show the superiority of the heritage to such views. Indoctrination sometimes fosters a fortress mentality, motivated by a fear of the dangerous ideas to be encountered outside the heritage. Furthermore, faithfulness to the heritage is sometimes equated with faithfulness to Christ; this means that any view which contests the heritage is unfaithful to Christ, and this leads to very intense reactions against people who hold those views. Many Southern Baptists sincerely believe that indoctrination is the best education.

The third view is that the best education is exploration. It agrees with the second view that education includes the transmission of a tradition, because it believes that the tradition contains truth which students need. This view also is open, however, to the presence of truth outside the tradition, even to those views which contest aspects of the tradition. It challenges students to develop a critical appreciation for the tradition and a critical appreciation for views contesting the tradition, and it entrusts them with the responsibility of deciding for themselves which view is truthful. This view does not see the clash of views as a conspiracy to subvert the truth, but as the honorable efforts of fallible human beings to understand the truth, a project which often exceeds everyone's grasp. And it does not equate unfaithfulness to the theological tradition with unfaithfulness to Christ or condemn those who do not accept all of the heritage as unfaithful Christians.

Many Southern Baptists sincerely believe that exploration is the best understanding of higher education. They feel that indoctrination does only half of the work which educators ought ideally to be doing. As much as they respect the traditions to be transmitted, they do not want to stop there, but to encourage students to explore beyond the boundaries of the tradition.

Finally, there is the view called relativization. This understanding of education sees little or no value in transmitting a tradition. The truth is to be found, it says, only in the interaction of our minds with the developing future, never in a heritage from the past. When the truth is found, it is unstable and apt to change; it is relative to the changing situation, not absolute and changeless. No one in Southern Baptist life holds this understanding of education.

Among Southern Baptists, then, the two live options in higher education are indoctrination—the transmission of a heritage only—and exploration—the transmission of a heritage together with an exploration of other resources in the quest for truth and understanding. Indoctrination necessarily excludes a factor which exploration necessarily includes. Both of these positions are held by responsible Southern Baptists.

Unfortunately, discussions about exploration and indoctrination can be misleading. On the one hand, those who are committed to education as exploration sometimes charge those committed to indoctrination with believing in brainwashing; it is an untrue accusation which has the effect of discrediting those who believe in indoctrination. On the other hand, those who believe in education as indoctrination sometimes charge those committed to exploration with believing in relativism; this too is an untrue accusation which has the effect of discrediting those who believe in exploration. These untrue accusations must be set aside in order for a meaningful engagement between the two views held by Southern Baptists to take place.

Baptists Should Participate in Ecumenism

Except for the Pentecostal and charismatic movements, the ecumenical movement, the movement toward Christian unity, is the most dramatic worldwide development in the church during the twentieth century. Ecumenism was born among Protestant missionaries; on the mission field, it did not make much sense to set up several varieties of Protestant churches among people who were unclear about what Christianity is. The Eastern Orthodox are very committed to ecumenism, and in the 1960s the Roman Catholic Church committed itself to ecumenism.

Southern Baptists resisted ecumenism early in the twentieth century. They helped organize the Baptist World Alliance as an alternative to groups such as the National Council of Churches in America and the World Council of Churches. They have continued to refuse to participate in most ecumenical organizations. There are some very limited exceptions. For example, the Convention participates in the International Sunday School Lesson program, and it has always been friendly to the American Bible Society. But the Convention has avoided most ties with non-Baptist organizations, including ecumenical ones.

However, a minority of Southern Baptists has been troubled by this. Their study of the New Testament passages which refer to the unity of Christ's followers, especially of the great prayer of Jesus for the unity of all his disciples in John 17, has led them to believe in the unity of all Christians and to be willing to express that belief in practical ways. They have come to believe that an important expression is through participation in ecumenical bodies.

But most Southern Baptists are not convinced. They feel that it is important for the Convention to continue to avoid entanglements with non-Baptists. This is the official position, but it is not quite the whole story. The Christian church has been changing in America, and some of the changes make it more difficult for Southern Baptists or anyone else not to encounter people in other denominations. Through Christian radio, television, and other media, many Southern Baptists have come to appreciate the work of non-Baptists such as James Dobson, Robert Schuller, and Chuck Swindoll.

The controversy in the Convention, therefore, is not so much between a conservative group who want to avoid contacts with non-Southern Baptists and a progressive group who want to make such contacts. It is rather between a conservative group who want to make contacts with one set of non-Baptists and a progressive group who want to make contacts with a different set of non-Baptists.

Here, then, are four views held by a minority of

Southern Baptists, and representative of the progressivist impulse: Women should be ordained to serve as pastors, the Bible should be studied critically, education should be exploration rather than indoctrination, and Baptists should participate in ecumenical movements.

Summary

Let us imagine a sun surrounded by six planets. The sun represents the beliefs held by the great majority of Southern Baptists until 1979, and the planets represent six clusters of beliefs held by important minorities in the Convention until 1979. In the following description of the majority tradition in Southern Baptist theology, the majority beliefs will be arranged and expressed in a way which represents how these beliefs are lived out in the life of a Baptist church and in the experiences of Baptist church members.

In the background of Southern Baptist beliefs are the ideas that there is one true God and that He created the world. The world has fallen into sin, so the Father sent the Son into the world to save sinners. Jesus Christ died for the sins of the world and rose again.

The greatest decision in every person's life is what to do about Jesus Christ. God wants everyone to be saved, and everyone can be saved by putting his or her faith in Jesus Christ.

Those who are saved are secure in the salvation which God gives them, and they can have complete assurance that their eternal home is heaven.

All those who are saved should participate actively in the life of a church. God has called the church to carry

out a world mission, and, with the help of the Holy
Spirit, the church can win the world to Christ. The most
important part of the church's work is missions and evangelism, and to carry these out, the church must preach
the gospel and work vigorously to persuade people to
respond to Christ with faith.

A true church is a believers church, comprising saved
persons who have been immersed in water in the name of
the Father, the Son, and the Holy Spirit. Those who have
been baptized thereby become members of the church
and may receive the Lord's Supper. Believers churches are
self-governing congregations, and they seek the will of
God without interference from anyone outside the congregation. All Christians are priests, and they make their
church decisions by democratic means. They also cooperate voluntarily with other congregations to carry out
missions, evangelism, education, and benevolences. The
churches should accept no support from government; the
Baptist ideal is a free church in a free state.

Christians confidently hope that in the future God
will complete the work which he has begun. The Bible is
God's written, authoritative Word to guide Christians in
their common faith and life, the only written revelation
given by God.

That is the sun, the majority tradition. We turn now
to the six planets rotating around it, the minority traditions.

One minority tradition is the Anabaptist. It reacts
against the church status of Southern Baptists and calls
them to return to a sect status, to resist the temptation to
be powerful in the ways of the world. It calls them to follow the teachings of Jesus in the Sermon on the Mount

and become pacifists. And it calls them to revise their understanding of justice; they are not to think of justice as the right to keep what one has earned, but as the responsibility to work for social arrangements by which every person has enough food, clothing, housing, education, and job opportunities to live a decent life.

A second minority tradition is the Calvinist; its concerns are related to salvation. This tradition calls Southern Baptists to a distinctive understanding of the sovereignty of God. It insists that, because people are dead in their sins, they are unable to make any response to the Gospel until after they have been born again. Calvinism reminds Southern Baptists of the biblical passages which suggest that God chooses some to be his people and rejects others. It asserts that upon the cross Christ intentionally atoned for the sins, not of the entire world, but only of those who are predestined to be saved. And it affirms God's sovereignty by saying that God acts with a grace which cannot finally be resisted.

A third minority tradition is the Landmark; its concerns are related to the church. It assures Baptists that Baptist churches are the only truly New Testament churches, and it calls them to dissociate themselves from those who baptize infants. It reminds them that the New Testament nowhere speaks of associations or conventions but only of local congregations, and it urges Southern Baptists to keep cooperation between local congregations to a minimum. One expression of this is to invite to the Lord's Supper only those who are members of the local congregation in which the Supper is being observed.

A fourth minority tradition is the deeper life; its concerns are for Christian living. It deals with the disap-

pointments which all sensitive Christians feel concerning
how they live their lives by saying that the problem is that
many Christians, even very informed and dedicated ones,
do not know the secret of Christian living. The secret is
that they must cease striving to live as faithful Christians
and begin instead to depend only upon God. When they
do this, God will work in their lives, and the result will be
lives that are always characterized by victory and happiness.

A fifth minority tradition is the fundamentalist.
Fundamentalism calls Southern Baptists not only to
believe in the fundamentals of the faith, and to teach and
practice them, but to defend them militantly against all
enemies, especially against liberalism. It urges them to
recognize that the original Hebrew and Greek manuscripts of the Bible, which no longer exist, were inerrant
in all matters including history and science as well as faith
and morals. It encourages Baptists to fill out their understanding of the end of the world with more than a basic
affirmation that the end is in God's hands; it calls for
affirmations concerning the tribulation, the millennium,
and the battle of Armageddon.

The last minority beliefs are untraditional proposals
for Southern Baptists to adopt several unrelated, new,
progressive activities. One is to ordain women to serve as
pastors of churches. Another is to use all the available
methods to study the Bible, including critical methods.
Another is to include in its institutions of higher education not only the transmission of the Baptist heritage but
also an encouragement for students to explore other traditions for themselves in a personal quest for truth and
understanding. The last is a call for Baptists to be

responsive to Christ's prayer for the unity of his disciples by entering into ecumenical relationships with all kinds of Christians.

That is a reconstruction of Southern Baptist theology as it was in the years leading up to 1979. It is our theological story. It is the way we were.

It is no longer the way we are.

PART THREE

THE WAY
WE MAY BECOME:
LOST TRADITIONS

CHAPTER 11

The Way We May Become: Lost Traditions

From the beginning this book has attempted to emphasize that the controversy in the Convention is a large, complex, social dislocation, and that it is difficult to interpret. It is even more difficult to predict what the theology of the new Southern Baptist Convention will be.

Nevertheless, we have had a decade and a half to get a sense of the theological concerns of the new leaders of the Convention. Many of the leaders are articulate spokesmen for their theological positions, and it is now possible to provide a tentative report on what they will offer Southern Baptists and what may well be accepted by the majority of Southern Baptists in the future.

This chapter discusses the aspects of the Southern Baptist majority tradition which are at risk in the new Southern Baptist Convention. Chapter 12 will indicate which aspects of the minority traditions will receive more emphasis in the new Convention than they did before 1979.

Beliefs Baptists Share with All Christians

The Southern Baptist majority tradition has been described in terms of four clusters of beliefs. The first is the beliefs which Southern Baptists share with all Christians. None of these eleven beliefs is at risk in the new Southern Baptist Convention.

This is a fact of surpassing importance. As indicated at the end of Chapter 1, I think that these are our most important beliefs. Far from being a lowest common denominator, they actually are a highest common denominator. The fact that the beliefs which Baptists share with other Christians are all intact after the controversy is the greatest cause for celebration in the new Convention insofar as theology is concerned.

This fact has a very important implication, namely, that, though Southern Baptists are now thoroughly polarized, they continue to have good theological resources for cooperation. If we believe that these common beliefs are more important than those which divide us, then we cannot say that we are polarized about our most important beliefs; the most that we can say is that we are polarized about some of our beliefs, though not about our most important ones. To this we should add concerning our present predicament that, as C. H. Dodd pointed out decades ago in a famous letter concerning ecumenism, often the most important factor in church divisions is not theology at all, but other factors such as a long history of distrust and conflict.[84]

Beliefs Baptists Share with Protestant Christians

The second cluster of beliefs in the Southern Baptist majority tradition is the Protestant beliefs. Here the issues are considerably more complicated.

The first of the Protestant beliefs, that the church must always be in the process of being reformed, is unaffected by the controversy in the Convention. No one has raised the question of whether or not the church must always be being reformed, and the new leaders of the Convention believe that, in providing a course correction for the Convention, they are practicing this Protestant principle.

The second of these beliefs, that the Bible alone is God's Word, also is unaffected by the controversy. This may come as a surprise to readers who have heard repeatedly that the controversy is about the Bible. However, what has been debated so heatedly is neither the universal Christian belief about whether the Bible is God's inspired Word and authoritative for Christian faith and practice, nor the Protestant belief that the authority of the Bible is superior to the authority of the church. What has been debated in the Southern Baptist Convention is whether the non-extant Hebrew and Greek autographs of the Bible are without errors in matters such as history and science as well as faith and morals. This controversial issue will be examined later in this book.

The third of these beliefs, *sola fide*, is now the subject of a heated debate among some conservative Protestants in the United States, and a few Southern Baptists have become involved in it. That debate is called the Lordship controversy, and the issue is whether or not a person must surrender totally to the Lordship of Christ in order to be saved. This controversy has not touched most Southern Baptists, and the two positions in that debate do not correspond to the two polarities in the Southern Baptist Convention. The belief that one is saved by God's grace through faith alone is not being publicly debated within the Southern Baptist Convention.

The fourth belief, that all Christians are secure in their salvation, is not now a part of the polarization of the Convention. However, for a brief period early in the controversy, it was. One of the most beloved of Southern Baptists' professional theologians was the late Dale Moody. Moody became convinced, entirely upon biblical evidence, that it is possible for a genuine Christian to commit apostasy and to cease to be a Christian. He indicated this in his systematic theology, *The Word of Truth,* as well as elsewhere. Nevertheless, this issue never became widely controversial, and the belief that Christians are secure in their faith may be expected to stand in the new Southern Baptist Convention. Thus, the first four Protestant beliefs are not at risk in the new Convention.

But the fifth Protestant belief, that all believers are priests, is a major factor in the polarization in the Convention, and the story is a very complicated one.

The New Testament does not provide a doctrine of the priesthood of believers; what it provides is an image of the priesthood of all believers. Because it is an image rather than a doctrine, its meaning is indeterminate, and it may be used to refer to any one of three ideas. It may be used to refer to the responsibilities of Christians as priests, to the privileges of Christians as priests, and to the freedom of Christians as priests. The biblical teaching concerning the priesthood of all God's people emphasized the privileges and responsibilities of that priesthood. In the sixteenth century Martin Luther emphasized the freedom of Christians as priests, and that is the controversial issue among Southern Baptists today. No one in the Convention has doubted whether Christians as priests are responsible to pray for one another, for example, or whether Christians as priests enjoy the privilege of access to God, for example. The controversial issue is the freedom of Christians as priests.

The controversy concerning the priesthood of believers has two parts. On the one hand, the old leaders of the Convention have understood the new leaders to be denying Christians their freedom as priests of God. On the other hand, the new leaders of the Convention have understood the old leaders to be asserting that, since all Christians are priests, one may believe whatever one likes and still be a good Baptist and Christian. We shall consider these two issues one at a time.

The old leaders have felt that the new leaders are infringing upon their liberties as Christians in several ways. Here are four examples.

An early example was the decision made by the Home Mission Board not to provide financial support for small mission churches that called women as their pastors. That seemed to be an interference with the freedom of congregations to call pastors of their choosing.

A second example is a tendency on the part of the new leaders to devalue the priesthood of all believers in favor of pastoral authority. This is very clear in a famous resolution which the Convention adopted at its meeting in San Antonio in 1988, which reads in part:

> Be it further RESOLVED. That the doc-
> trine of the Priesthood of the Believer in
> no way contradicts the biblical under-
> standing of the role, responsibility, and
> authority which is seen in the command
> to the local church in Hebrews 13:17.
> "Obey your leaders, and submit to
> them."[85]

Many of the old leaders feel that this call to submit to
pastors amounted to a denial of the Baptist commitment
to congregational decision-making through democratic
processes.

A third example is the commitment of many of the
new leaders to voluntary, state-sponsored prayer in public
schools and to parental choice; parental choice is the idea
that the government should provide vouchers for parents
so that they can send their children to whatever school
they choose, including schools in which religion is
taught. Many of the old leaders felt that these practices
constitute a rejection of the Baptist commitment to the
separation of church and state, and therefore a violation
of the freedom of Americans who do not believe in the
religious practices which the government would be supporting.

A fourth example is the willingness of the Convention
to provide an authorized interpretation of particular biblical texts. An important example of this is the report
which the peace committee of the Convention made in
1987. Referring to a phrase in Article I of *The Baptist
Faith and Message*, the report says:

We, as a Peace Committee, have found that most Southern Baptists see "truth without any mixture of error for its matter," as meaning, for example, that

(1) They believe in direct creation of mankind and therefore they believe Adam and Eve were real persons.

(2) They believe the named authors did indeed write the biblical books attributed to them by those books.

(3) They believe the miracles described in Scripture did indeed occur as supernatural events in history.

(4) They believe that the historical narratives given by biblical authors are indeed accurate and reliable as given by those authors.[86]

Two pages later we read:

We call upon Southern Baptist institutions to recognize the great number of Southern Baptists who believe this interpretation of Article I of the Baptist Faith and Message Statement of 1963, and, in the future, to build their professional staffs and faculties from those who clearly reflect such dominant convictions and beliefs held by Southern Baptists at large.[87]

These findings amount to formal, official interpretations of four quite specific groups of texts in the Bible.

They are not very detailed interpretations, and most Southern Baptists probably would agree with the interpretations, but they are nevertheless formal, official interpretations. Many of the old leaders of the Convention regard this document as an infringement of their freedom as priests to interpret the Bible for themselves.

Here, then, are four occasions on which the old leaders, appealing to the priesthood of believers, resist the infringement of their liberties: the freedom of congregations to call their pastors without interference, the freedom of congregations to act democratically to discern God's will without authoritarian pastors, the freedom of all Americans not to be taxed to support religious practices, and the freedom of all Christians to interpret the Bible for themselves.

I will deal with all four of these issues in due time. Here I want to make a proposal concerning how we handle issues related to freedom.

First, it is understandable that Luther, in his reaction against oppressive practices in the Roman Catholic Church, would use the priesthood of believers to assert the freedom of all Christians to have general access to God. I believe that Luther's position about access to God is correct. However, I do not think that it gains any authority by appealing to the biblical image of the priesthood of believers, because the Bible does not do so. The biblical texts about priesthood are not affirmations concerning freedom of access, and the biblical texts about access to God, such as Romans 5:1, do not employ the image of the priesthood of believers.

My proposal, then, is that issues such as the four listed above should be dealt with without reference to the biblical image of the priesthood of believers.

The concern of the new leaders of the Convention is that the image of the priesthood of believers has been used to mean that anyone is entitled to believe anything whatsoever and still have the right to be considered a good Christian and a good Baptist. This idea has been voiced repeatedly in the years since 1979, and it is difficult to know how to deal with it. I have attempted to locate examples of this claim in the writings of the old leaders, but without success. I was especially hopeful that recent books by Walter Shurden and William Tuck and an earlier essay by Cecil Sherman might provide an example, but they did not. Shurden makes a strong case that freedom is intrinsic to the Baptist identity, but he insists that freedom must always be balanced by responsibility.[88] Tuck says that some people have seen the doctrine of the priesthood of believers as "authorizing any private interpretation, which a person may have, no matter how uninformed or isolated from the body of Christian believers that person may be," but he says that this view of the priesthood of believers is incorrect.[89] Sherman makes a passionate and eloquent plea for the complete freedom of all Christians to interpret the Bible, but he nowhere suggests that this freedom entitles the interpreter to arrive at any conclusion whatever and still have the right to claim to be a good Christian or Baptist.[90] While it is quite possible that some Baptists have claimed that the priesthood of believers entitles them to believe whatever they wish, my tentative judgment is that no one has actually taken this position and so the new leaders do not need to worry about it anymore.

This image concerning the priesthood of believers is

used very differently by the new leaders of the Convention than by the old leaders, and the new leaders are not as enthusiastic about the image as the old leaders were. It will not continue to exercise the influence in the new Convention which it did in the years leading up to 1979.

How, then, does the new Southern Baptist Convention stand on the beliefs which Baptists have shared with Protestant Christians? The first four beliefs are intact: The church must always be in the process of being reformed, the Bible alone is the Word of God, salvation is by God's grace through faith alone, and all believers are secure in their salvation. For this we may be thankful.

However, in the new Southern Baptist Convention, the fifth belief, the priesthood of all believers, will receive less emphasis than it did before 1979, because the new leaders of the Convention understand it to be in conflict with some of their beliefs such as pastoral authority.

Beliefs which are Unique to Baptists

A description of the beliefs which are unique to Baptists includes eight beliefs. The first three of these beliefs have not been factors in the controversy, and we may expect them to be retained in the new Southern Baptist Convention. They are believers baptism, by immersion, resulting in a believers church.

Each of the other five beliefs has been a factor in the controversy. The first is the autonomy of local congregations. In principle, all Baptist congregations are entirely self-governing. No bishop or synod can tell a local congregation what decisions to make. But, as noted briefly in Chapter 3, there are some complicating factors. One is that the denomination does, in fact, exert influence upon the decisions made by local congregations by general activities such as publishing literature. Even so, this does not alter the fundamental commitment to autonomy, which is that, when the chips are down, the decisions concerning the life of a congregation will be made by its members only, not by any outsiders.

The other complicating factor concerns the participation of congregations in local associations, state conventions, and the Southern Baptist Convention. Here it should be noted that Baptists practice what they call a non-connectional polity; that is, it is not necessary for a congregation to belong to its local association in order to be a member of the state convention, or for it to belong to the association or state convention in order to be a member of the Southern Baptist Convention. In practice, of course, almost all congregations belong to the three entities mentioned, but this is not required.

As might be expected, associations, state conventions, and the national Convention set the boundaries of their membership; they decide which congregations may and which may not be members. This selection process seems to put them in conflict with local church autonomy.

Here are three examples. First, some years ago the First Baptist Church of Oklahoma City was evicted from the local association because of its willingness to ordain women as deacons. Second, the Prescott Memorial Baptist Church of Memphis was evicted from its local association and from the Tennessee Baptist Conviction because it called a woman, Nancy Hastings Sehested, as pastor. Third, two churches in North Carolina were evicted from the Southern Baptist Convention because one of them supported a homosexual in his intention to become a minister and the other gave its blessing to the commitment of two homosexuals to live together.

How autonomous, many people ask, are these local churches, if associations and conventions are able to evict congregations in this way? At first blush it would seem that these evictions do constitute an abridgement of the autonomy of these local congregations.

On reflection, however, it seems that this is not the case, for this reason. Any group—an association or a convention included—can exist only if it has boundaries; if there are no boundaries, there is no group. It is perfectly appropriate that a group set its own boundaries, and that is what Baptist associations and conventions do. One may not agree with the decisions of the groups to evict the churches described above, but it is difficult to find any reason to say that the associations and the conventions were not entitled to set the boundaries of their group.

It is especially difficult to say that their doing so constituted an infringement of the autonomy of the local churches. No committees or officers from the associations or conventions met with the congregations and attempted to get them to reverse their decisions. The groups simply decided that, as long as the congregations retained their convictions or practices, they could not belong to their respective associations or conventions. My conclusion, therefore, is that the setting of boundaries for membership by associations and conventions is an appropriate practice which does not infringe upon the autonomy of local congregations.

There are also two subsidiary issues here. One is whether the decisions which are being made about boundaries in the new Southern Baptist Convention are wise ones. Some of them may be unwise, but the wisdom of the decisions is not the issue here; the issue is whether the making of decisions in and of itself constitutes a repudiation of the Baptist heritage of local church autonomy, and it does not.

The other subsidiary issue is whether there is a more strict policing of the boundaries of the Convention now than in the past. The answer is that there is. In the past, policing was rare and informal. Local associations were almost the only entities to police their boundaries, and they did so with very great reserve, on very few occasions. Now a great deal more policing is going on, at the local, state, and national levels, and there is no reason to think that it will diminish in the new Southern Baptist Convention.

Nevertheless, these activities do not in themselves constitute an infringement of the autonomy of local congregations. So I would add this fourth uniquely Baptist belief to be added to the list of those which are likely to remain unchanged in the future.

The fifth distinctively Baptist belief is that local congregations should seek the will of God by democratic processes under the Lordship of Christ. In the resolution on the priesthood of believers which was adopted in 1988, the Convention used a biblical text which says, "Obey your leaders, and submit to them." In the final analysis, obedience to pastors is not compatible with congregational decision-making by democratic processes. Efforts may be made to tone down the stark contrast between these two forms of church government, but in the end they are not reconcilable. One cannot avoid the question of who has the final word; either it is the pastor alone, or it is the congregation acting together.

The traditional Baptist belief has been that the authority to make decisions rests finally with the people, under God, of course. That is quite clear in *The Baptist Faith and Message* (VI):

> This church is an autonomous body, operating through democratic processes under the Lordship of Jesus Christ. In such a congregation members are equally responsible.

It is clear that at least some of the new leaders of the Convention do not accept this view.

In fairness, let it be said again here that the New Testament nowhere prescribes a form of church government. That is why Christians have followed several forms of church government, and they have justifiably pointed to biblical antecedents for each of them. The new leaders who intend to assert the authority of a pastor to make the final decision for his congregation naturally call upon New Testament texts in support of their view. This is perfectly appropriate.

In the new Southern Baptist Convention the commitment to the traditional Baptist practice of congregational decision-making is being eroded, and, unless this trend is reversed, the practice will be lost in many congregations.

The sixth uniquely Baptist belief is that local congregations, though autonomous, should cooperate with each other. Though it is a complicated issue, we shall deal with it only briefly.

The complication arises because cooperation is an imprecise term. How exactly does one measure the co-operation of one congregation with others?

The traditional Southern Baptist way to do this is in terms of financial contributions made by the congregation to the institutions of the Convention such as the mission boards. Since 1925 that has taken the specific form of money contributed to the central funding mechanism called the Cooperative Program. In itself this clearly is not a satisfactory definition of cooperation, as a very uncooperative church might send in donations and a very cooperative one might have little or no money to contribute. Nevertheless, contributing to the Cooperative Program is the conventional way of measuring cooperation.

One unprovable generalization describes what is happening concerning cooperation in the new Convention. Because it is a generalization, there are, of course, many exceptions.

What seems to be happening is this: Until 1979, the Convention invariably chose as its leaders pastors who had led their churches to contribute generously to Convention causes. However, now that those pastors are no longer elected as the leaders of the Convention, they tend not to lead their churches to be as cooperative as they once were.

Conversely, before the new leaders were in charge of the Convention, some of them tended not to lead their churches to be very cooperative with the Convention. One might assume that now that they are in charge, they will lead their churches to be more cooperative. As it turns out, however, it is too early to see if they will do this successfully. Churches with a long history of spending their money only on their local ministries may need a great deal of time to come to appreciate the value of sending it to a common fund to support ministries which are not local.[91]

If this generalization is true (even allowing for a great many exceptions), it follows that there will be a decline in the funding of the Cooperative Program, or at least in the rate of growth of that funding. That decline is already visible, and, unless the new leaders succeed in leading their churches to give far more generously than they have until now, it probably will continue. The decline, incidentally, is matched by a similar decline in the central funding agencies of almost all of the large denominations in America, so the new leaders will be fighting against a general trend in American religion.

The conclusion, therefore, is that the sixth distinctly Baptist belief, that autonomous churches ought to cooperate to carry out ministries together, is in principle unchanged in the new Southern Baptist Convention, but the degree of cooperation is declining and will continue to decline unless the new leaders can reverse a trend toward congregations' spending more of their money on local ministries and sending less to the Cooperative Program.

The seventh distinctively Baptist belief is that church and state should be separate. It is a belief which is clearly spelled out in *The Baptist Faith and Message* (XVII).

> Church and state should be separate....
> The church should not resort to the civil

> power to carry on its work. . . . The state
> has no right to impose religious penalties
> of any kind. . . . A free church in a free
> state is the Christian ideal.

This is an interesting series of statements. The first and last sentences contain two of the slogans of the traditional Baptist position: separation of church and state, and a free church in a free state. The two middle sentences are exactly parallel to the two religion clauses of the First Amendment to the Constitution of the United States: "Congress shall make no law respecting an establishment of religion or prohibiting the free exercise thereof."

The new leaders of the Convention understand the relationship between church and government differently than the old leaders did. Although some of the new leaders of the Convention have made statements which belittle the separation of church and state, these are not the important indicators that changes are occurring. The important indicators are actions which have been taken by the Convention and commitments which have been made by agencies of the Convention. I mention just two.

In 1991 in Atlanta, the Convention adopted a resolution that affirmed the right of parents to educate their children according to their religious convictions. The resolution approved of "choice in education initiatives which include proper tax incentives for families," and then affirmed that it is possible for these initiatives to be fully consistent with the First Amendment prohibition against any governmental establishment of religion. In plain language, the resolution affirmed that it is appropriate for government to provide vouchers for children's education in schools which promote religion, and it said that this is not a form of government support of religion.

A second example concerns state-sponsored prayer in public schools. The Christian Life Commission of the Southern Baptist Convention is committed to the principle that school teachers and guest speakers may lead children in prayer in public schools, provided participation in such prayers be kept voluntary.[92] These actions are reversals of the understanding of separation of church and state which has prevailed in the Convention in the past.

In defense of the new leaders, let me say that it often is very difficult to do justice to both the no-establishment clause and the free-exercise clause. For example, it seems to be a state-sponsored religious activity if a teacher is allowed to lead her students in prayer, but it seems to be an abridgement of her free exercise of her religion if she is prohibited from doing so. Similarly, it seems an establishment of religious practices for the government to provide vouchers to fund religious education, but it seems a denial of the free exercise of religion to Christian parents not to fund their children's religious education in exactly the same way the education of the children of parents with no religion is funded in public schools which are neutral toward religion.

But, even allowing for the fact that it is sometimes difficult to know the best way to draw the line between the principles of no-establishment and free exercise of religion, it is clear that the new leaders of the Convention will draw it quite differently than it has been drawn in the past. They share the traditional Baptist concern about free exercise, but the new leaders have decidedly less concern about the establishment issue than Baptists had in the past. In their support for vouchers and for voluntary, state-sponsored prayer in public schools, they are committing the Convention to do precisely what is forbidden in *The Baptist Faith and Message* (XVII): "The church should not resort to the civil power to carry on its work."

The conclusion, then, is that this great Baptist principle is being revised so that in the new Convention it will not exist as we have known it. The new Convention will accept government support for religious practices which would have been rejected by the Convention before 1979.

The eighth distinctive Baptist belief is that confessions of faith which are descriptive of the faith of the people are useful, but creeds, which are employed prescriptively, are wrong; the Bible is the only creed of the Baptists. Two events have demonstrated that in the new Southern Baptist Convention this part of the Baptist heritage is at risk. One is the case of Dale Moody; the other is the report of the peace committee.

Dale Moody spent his life teaching theology at Southern Baptist Theological Seminary. Since the founding of the seminary by James P. Boyce, all of its faculty have agreed in writing to teach in accordance with and not contrary to a brief document called the "Abstract of Principles." The document, like *The Baptist Faith and Message*, says quite clearly that Christians cannot lose their salvation. Dale Moody dissented from that view, as we have seen, and in his classes at Southern Seminary he said that the New Testament teaches that Christians can forfeit their salvation. When asked about this, Moody explained that from the beginning of his tenure at the seminary he had indicated to the proper seminary officials that he did not agree with the document on this one point.

The question is whether the use which the seminary made of the Abstract of Principles is consistent with the Baptist tradition which accepts descriptive confessions but rejects prescriptive creeds. It seems to me that it does not, for the document at Southern Seminary is used not only to describe the view of Boyce and others but to prescribe what professors may and may not teach, and that means it is used in a creedal way. The five other seminaries have made similar use of various documents.

How can this be handled? There seem to be three possible alternatives.

One is to renounce our Baptist tradition that confessions are wise and that creeds are unwise. Our Baptist forebears were wise to resist prescriptive creeds.

Another is to say that the Convention generally and the trustees of the schools in particular have no right to place any constraints upon teachers. I am unwilling to do that either The Convention operates the schools in order to carry out certain purposes, and the Convention is therefore entitled to place constraints upon the teachers in the schools.

The only alternative seems to be a pragmatic one. It is to recognize that, while the Baptist ideal is to have descriptive confessions and not prescriptive creeds, it is not possible to live up to that ideal in the schools owned by the Convention. In schools, it is regrettably necessary to place constraints upon teachers, and this amounts to creedalism. The unbaptistic effect of this may be mitigated somewhat by using phrases such as "teach in accordance with and not contrary to" the document, but the practice still falls below the Baptist ideal. That is not a pleasant truth, but it is Christian realism, as Reinhold Niebuhr might say, and we can learn to live with it.

Dale Moody is the hard case because he was so deeply committed to the majority tradition of Southern Baptists and such an energetic champion of that tradition, except on this single issue. The matter would be much simpler in the case of a professor with little or no appreciation for the majority tradition.

It also would be simpler in the case of an issue on which a seminary's document says nothing. That was the situation in the decade of the 1960s, when many professors took a very unpopular stand on relations between the races; they suffered for their stand in some cases, but they were not teaching anything contrary to the documents of their schools.

The second event which alerts us to the fact that the principle of having no creed but the Bible is at risk, is the report of the peace committee. That report, as stated earlier, provides interpretations of four groups of Bible passages. The interpretations offered are limited, but they are formal and they are official.

The question, then, is whether the existence of formal, official interpretations of the Bible constitutes an interference with the traditional Baptist principle of having no creed but the Bible. The answer, simply, is that it does. It follows that those churches who treasure the principle most deeply ought to avoid as much as possible the practice of providing official interpretations.

"As much as possible." The question is, have Southern Baptists ever offered official interpretations of Scripture? They had not done so in a formal way before 1987. However, in many informal ways they have offered interpretations of many Scripture texts. For example, the adoption of confessions is a de facto interpretation of Scripture; for that matter, the publication of any book or piece of literature by the official press of the Convention constitutes an informal official interpretation of the Bible. It is not possible, so far as I can tell, to avoid informal interpretations of Scripture.

Nor is it desirable. It is appropriate and necessary for a religious group to confess its faith, and, in the case of Christian groups, that entails offering more or less official interpretations of Scripture.

On the other hand, what was done in the report of the peace committee was unprecedented in Baptist life. It is a very small step from that report to the Convention's saying, "Unless you accept these interpretations of these texts, we will not allow you to be a Southern Baptist." And that, quite simply, is creedalism and the loss of the Baptist heritage which has resisted creedalism.

Therefore, a major change in the new Southern Baptist Convention is its apparent willingness to sacrifice the Baptist tradition of having no creed but the Bible in favor of the offering of formal, official interpretations of Scripture. The evidence for this is much clearer in the case of the peace committee report than in the constraints placed upon seminary professors.

Incidentally, the adoption of formal, official interpretations of Scripture is not consistent with what many of the new leaders themselves have been saying since 1979.

From the beginning of the controversy they have said repeatedly that the problem in the Convention is not different interpretations of the Bible but different views of the Bible, inerrancy and non-inerrancy. The peace committee report makes it clear that at least part of the problem is different interpretations.

In conclusion, of the eight uniquely Baptist beliefs, it appears that five will remain unchanged in the new Southern Baptist Convention: Baptism will be for believers only, by immersion only; churches will be believers churches. Though associations and conventions will police their member congregations more rigorously than in the past, churches will continue to enjoy autonomy. Congregations will still, in principle if not as fully in practice, be committed to cooperation with each other.

The other three uniquely Baptist beliefs will disappear or be radically altered in the new Convention. A move will be made away from congregational decision making toward decision making by pastors. The wall of separation between church and state will be lowered in favor of more government support of religious activities in places such as schools. The principle of providing descriptive confessions of faith but refusing to provide prescriptive creeds will be effectively jettisoned, and creedalism will no longer be portrayed as an evil as it was before 1979.

Beliefs Baptists Share with Revivalist Christians

Southern Baptists share four beliefs with other Christians who have been influenced by the great revivals of the eighteenth century. They are the need for every person to undergo a conversion, the need for all converts to have a full assurance of their salvation, the priority of evangelism in the church's task, and the priority of missions in the church's work. None of these four beliefs has been an issue in the controversy, and the new Convention is likely to continue its commitment to each of them. Since these beliefs are the center of gravity for many Baptists, it is not surprising that they have been unaffected by the controversy.

Conclusion

The majority tradition of Southern Baptists comprises four clusters of beliefs, a total of twenty-seven beliefs. Of these twenty-seven, the four which are going to be lost or drastically altered in the new Convention are the Protestant belief in the priesthood of all Christians and the distinctively Baptist beliefs in congregational decision-making, the separation of church and state, and the practice of having no creed but the Bible.

The loss of the four traditions is regrettable.

The restricted meaning and diminished importance of the priesthood of believers is unfortunate. However, it is not a tragedy because all of the biblical usages of the image are still intact. Also, the strongest case for the various freedoms is a case made without reference to the image of the priesthood of believers.

The loss of congregational decision making by democratic means is a tragedy. Democracy is not efficient, and it is not a foolproof way for a congregation to discern God's will. Nevertheless, the use of democratic means for arriving at decisions does more to insure that the dignity of all members is respected than any other means, and it calls forth the best from people because it is they, and no one else including their pastor, who are responsible for the decisions which affect the life of the congregation. Further, there is every reason to believe that a congregation of intentional believers is just as able to discern God's will as any individual, since the congregation brings to decision making the wisdom gained through the cumulative experiences of all its members. The loss of this Baptist principle in the new Southern Baptist Convention will be regretted.

The loss of the principle of the separation of church and state is the greatest tragedy in the history of Southern Baptist Convention.[93] The separation of church and state has been one of the most successful components of the American experiment. The state has held together without the glue of an official religion, and the church has flourished without the support of the state.

As government provides increased support for religious activities, more and more Americans will come to associate religion with government and therefore to feel the kind of contempt toward religion which they now feel toward government. In spite of the scandals in the personal lives of some religious leaders in recent years, the American people continue to have vastly more respect for the churches than they do for their government; that will change as the government becomes more involved in religious practices. It has happened in Europe, where churches are officially established, and it will happen here where government support will be just as real though less obvious. And the irony is that religious people such as the new Southern Baptist leaders, instead of opposing this change, are welcoming it enthusiastically. They have

made a tragic mistake which will have destructive conse-
quences for the nation, for the Convention, and for the
Christian cause in America.

The fourth belief which is being lost in the new
Convention, the principle of having no creed but the
Bible, is also tragic. It is very difficult to explain to people who have not experienced it how Baptists have managed to remain unified without recourse to prescriptive
creeds. They have been held together by their beliefs,
among other things, just as all religious groups are, but,
unlike other groups, they stayed together without a prescriptive creed. Because they had no prescriptive creed,
they have handled theological differences in an *ad hoc*
manner, as they arose. It is a messy arrangement, not a
neat one, and it is difficult to explain to outsiders how it
works. But it has worked and it might have continued to
work in the future. It will not be given a chance to work
in the new Convention.

Does the loss of these four beliefs mean that the new
Convention will be more conservative than the
Convention was before 1979? Quite the contrary. To be
conservative is to know, love, and transmit your traditions. In the new Convention, four valuable beliefs will
be lost from the Southern Baptist heritage, a fact which
conservatives must regret.

The following chapter provides an examination of the
six minority traditions to see which of these are likely to
become part of the majority tradition in the new
Convention.

CHAPTER 12

The Way We May Become: Innovations

Many innovations may be introduced in the new Southern Baptist Convention, including many theological innovations, and some of them may be unrelated to any of the six clusters of beliefs held by minorities in the Convention before 1979. Some observers think that they have already seen such theological innovations. For example, they notice shifts in attitude toward charismatic practices and toward some forms of worship.

However, this concluding chapter will be restricted to speaking of changes which are related to the themes already dealt with in this book. The beliefs held by the six minority groups before 1979 will be reviewed pointing out which of these beliefs are held by the new leaders of the Convention and so are candidates for the new majority tradition.

Anabaptist Beliefs

The three Anabaptist beliefs that were reviewed were the proposal that Southern Baptists should move away from their church-type status in society and become a sect-type group; that they should take more seriously Jesus' words in the Sermon on the Mount and become pacifists; and that they should revise their understandings of justice away from the idea that justice is an individual's right to keep what he has made in favor of the idea that justice is the right of all persons to have decent food, clothing, housing, education, and job opportunities.

The new leaders of the Convention have shown no interest in any of these ideas. The new Southern Baptist Convention is likely to be less hospitable to the Anabaptist tradition than the old Convention was.

Calvinist Beliefs

The description of the Calvinist beliefs followed a traditional procedure. The TULIP acronym is used as a summary of the beliefs of the Synod of Dort held in Holland in 1619, to describe the proposals made by an organized and articulate minority of Southern Baptists. The fifth of these, the perseverance of the saints, is a part of the majority tradition of Southern Baptists. It is likely to remain so in the new Convention. The other four beliefs are the total depravity of human beings, God's unconditional election of some (and not of others) to be saved, an understanding of the cross of Christ which says that God intended it to atone for the sins of the elect only, and an understanding of God's grace as finally irresistible.

These four beliefs function as a cluster; they more or less stand or fall together. In fact, logically it would seem that the same is true of the perseverance of the saints. Southern Baptists may be the only group to have isolated perseverance from the other Calvinistic beliefs and retained it while rejecting or radically revising the others.

Will this cluster of Calvinist beliefs become a part of the majority tradition in the new Southern Baptist Convention? It is not possible to know, and the reason is that the new leaders of the Convention are divided about Calvinism. Some of the new leaders are firmly committed to Calvinism and to restoring it to the role in Southern Baptist life which it had in the era of James Boyce and John Dagg. Others of the new leaders are just as vigorously opposed to Calvinism.

This is an issue which the leaders will be sorting out in the years ahead. It is impossible to tell how it will turn out.

Even if the new leaders decide to move the Convention toward Calvinism, it probably will be a very long time before these ideas are known and understood, let alone accepted, by the majority of Southern Baptists. Many Southern Baptists, like many other Protestants today, feel intuitively that Calvinism is a form of determinism. And Southern Baptists intuitively associate their commitment to evangelism and missions with a belief that all who hear the Gospel—not just those who are elect—are entirely free to accept it if only they will.

Therefore, whatever the new leaders decide, for the foreseeable future, it is likely that the majority tradition in the new Southern Baptist Convention will not include rigorous Calvinism.

Landmark Beliefs

The summary of the Landmark minority tradition includes two themes. The first is that Baptists should separate from non-Baptists because non-Baptists have been unfaithful to the New Testament. The second is that local Baptist congregations should keep their cooperation with each other to a minimum. The reason is that the New Testament authorizes only one institution, the local congregation, and other structures such as boards of missions and publication are human creations with no biblical precedent. One expression of the noncooperation of local congregations is that only members of the local congregation may participate in the Lord's Supper when the congregation observes it.

The first Landmark belief probably will not become part of the new majority tradition. Like the old leaders, the new leaders often make common cause with non-Baptists rather than dissociating from them. For example, the Christian Life Commission now works closely with non-Baptist groups to oppose abortion, and the new leaders of the Convention invite non-Baptists to address the Convention.

The second belief is that local congregations should restrict the size of denominational organizations. None of the new leaders of the Convention has expressed any interest in reducing the size or influence of the denominational structures. Doubtless they are as concerned as the past leaders were about the problems which accompany large, bureaucratic organizations. In fact, they occasionally referred to the bureaucratic problems during their controversy with the old leaders.[94] But they have not indicated a desire to eliminate the large organizations. Nor have they expressed any interest in reopening the issue of communion. It seems likely that the Convention will remain unchanged on this issue also.

The Landmark beliefs are no more likely to become part of the majority tradition in the new Convention than they were before 1979.

Deeper Life Beliefs

The deeper life beliefs are that many Christians do not know how to live life victoriously; that there is a secret to living a victorious life; that the secret is to depend upon God rather than strive to live responsibly; and that those who do this live lives that will be happy and victorious.

The new leaders of the Convention seem to be divided on the deeper life beliefs just as they are on the Calvinist beliefs. Some of the new leaders hold this understanding of Christian living and others do not.[95] The new leaders will have to sort out whether or not they will promote these beliefs among Southern Baptists more fully than they have been promoted in the past.

Unlike the Calvinist beliefs, however, it is possible for an attenuated version of one or two of these beliefs to succeed without the entire cluster becoming part of the new majority tradition. For example, it could happen that in the years ahead, much more will be said about a secret of Christian living than was said in the past; the seminaries and the denominational literature could alert many Southern Baptists to the idea that striving to live faithfully is doomed to fail, and that what is needed is dependence upon God rather than striving. All of this might conceivably happen, for example, without the tendency toward perfectionism becoming as dominant in the Convention as it is in the deeper life tradition.

What this means, then, is that it is not possible to predict whether any or all of these beliefs will become part of the majority tradition of the new Convention.

Fundamentalist Beliefs

Chapter 9 described three beliefs held in the fundamentalist movement early in the twentieth century. One is that true Christians should militantly oppose liberalism. The second is that the original Hebrew and Greek manuscripts of the Bible were inerrant not only in their teachings about Christian faith and life but also in their teachings about all other issues including science and history. The third is that Christ is going to return suddenly and literally to the earth and reign for a thousand years.

These three beliefs now prevail in the new Southern Baptist Convention.

The controversy was itself an example of the new leaders' putting the first principle into practice, and they will continue to do so. It is not clear how intense the militancy will be in the future or whether militancy will be directed toward views other than progressive ones. In principle, the Convention could begin militant opposition toward, for examples, Calvinism or the charismatic movement. In 1992 and 1993 the Convention had skirmishes with a new group of teachings, those of Masonry, and the militant opposition to Masonry failed at the 1993 Convention. This is a hopeful sign, for militancy is always destructive of community and cooperation. It is not difficult to imagine Southern Baptists who are Masons becoming quite alienated from the Convention if the Convention had adopted a more militant position on Masonry. If the level of militancy is reduced in the future, the cooperation and sense of community in the Convention will benefit. Of course, the desire for community in and cooperation with the Convention was lost long ago for many people who were hurt in the controversy. But it is important for the millions of Christians who remain within the Convention, both literally and emotionally, that militancy not remain a permanent feature of the life of the Convention.

The second issue concerns the Bible. From the beginning of the controversy, the new leaders have said that the issue with which they were most concerned was the truthfulness of the Bible. When asked to explain what that meant, they said, almost without exception, that the original Hebrew and Greek manuscripts of the Bible were without error of any sort in all matters, including science and history as well as faith and practice. There will be no retreat from this position.

What is not so clear is whether, in the new Convention, much effort will be made to communicate the technicalities of this view of the inerrancy of the non-extant Hebrew and Greek manuscripts to all Southern Baptists. The technicalities have not been emphasized in the controversy, and they may receive little emphasis in the new Convention. However, the teaching of the technicalities of inerrancy got off to a running start with the publication of *The Doctrine of the Bible* by David S. Dockery as the Convention's study book for 1992.

The commitment of the new leaders to the dispensa-

tional version of premillennial eschatology is public
knowledge, but there has been less said about this issue
than the two earlier issues.[96] Nevertheless, this scenario
for the end of the world will probably be promoted vigorously in the new Southern Baptist Convention.

All three of the beliefs of fundamentalism either
already have become or will become in the near future a
part of the majority tradition in the new Southern Baptist
Convention.

Progressive Beliefs

Chapter 10 looked at four progressive beliefs: the
ordaining of women to serve as pastors, the critical study
of the Bible, higher education as exploration rather than
indoctrination, and ecumenism. Those who held these
beliefs were often frustrated at the unresponsiveness of
the Convention prior to 1979. In a sense, their frustration may be coming to an end, not because the new
Convention is going to accept their proposals, but
because the new leaders of the Convention have rejected
them so vigorously that it is now clear to everyone that
the progressive beliefs have no future in the new Southern
Baptist Convention.

The Convention rejected the ordination of women to
serve as pastors in the decision of the Home Mission
Board not to fund mission churches which call women as
pastors. It rejected the critical study of the Bible in the
report of the peace committee. Its course correction for
the seminaries is a project of shifting them from their earlier commitment to theological exploration toward a
commitment to theological indoctrination.

The fourth progressive belief, in the importance of ecumenism, is a little more complicated. The new leaders of the Convention have little interest in strengthening ecumenical ties with some of the groups with whom the old leaders worked to strengthen ties. For example, a cycle of nine years of conversations between Roman Catholic and Southern Baptist scholars, funded on the Baptist side by the Home Mission Board, came to an end just a year or so after the Home Mission Board elected a new president.

On the other hand, the new leaders have ecumenical commitments of their own, and they probably will lead the Convention to share in some of those commitments. The new leaders participate regularly on boards and committees with persons and groups which are identified as religiously and politically conservative. The building of bridges between the new leaders of the Convention and persons such as Jerry Falwell, James Dobson, Franky Schaeffer, and Chuck Swindoll, probably will continue.

The conclusion is that the majority tradition of the new Southern Baptist Convention will not include the ordination of women to serve as pastors, the critical study of the Bible, or the development of higher education as exploration rather than indoctrination. The majority tradition will include a new ecumenism, an ecumenism with conservative religious and political groups, of which those led by Jerry Falwell may be representative.

Conclusion

To summarize my interpretation of the theology of the new Southern Baptist Convention, its majority tradition is likely to omit or dramatically alter four beliefs which were part of the majority tradition before 1979.

[1] The new majority tradition will no longer speak of the priesthood of all believers with reference to Christian freedom. It may not include any reference to this belief at all, or, more likely, it may employ this belief to refer to the responsibilities and privileges of Christians, but the usage which has been traditional since Martin Luther of employing the image of priesthood to speak of Christian freedom will decline or disappear.

[2] The new majority tradition will no longer include congregational decision making under Christ's Lordship by democratic means. The authority of a pastor to make his congregation's decisions and the responsibility of other church members to follow their pastor loyally, will displace congregational decision making.

[3] The new majority tradition will no longer include a vigorous commitment to the separation of church and state. The phrase itself may be rejected, as it has been by some of the new leaders. More likely, the phrase will endure but will be reinterpreted to mean principally that government should not interfere with religious groups; the traditional view that "the church should not resort to the civil power to carry on its work," will be displaced as the Convention works for voluntary, state-sponsored prayer in public schools and for government-provided vouchers for funding religious schools.

[4] The new majority tradition will no longer include a resistance to prescriptive creeds. The new leaders of the Convention do not share the conviction of earlier Baptists that creeds are pernicious.[97]

In addition, the majority tradition in the new Convention is likely to include three new beliefs.

[1] A militant opposition to what has been perceived to be liberal theology has been a major factor in the formation of the new Southern Baptist Convention, and that militancy will continue in the future. It is not clear whether the militancy will be directed toward other kinds of beliefs, nor is it clear how extensive the destruction of community and cooperation will be.

[2] In the new Convention, the majority beliefs about the Bible will no longer be simply the universal Christian belief that it is God's uniquely inspired, authoritative Word, and the Protestant belief that it is superior to all creeds and traditions. The new majority view will be that the original, non-extant Hebrew and Greek manuscripts of the Bible were without error in any matters whatsoever, including science and history as well as faith and practice. It is not clear how carefully this will be taught.

[3] In the new Convention, the dispensational, premillennial understanding of the end of the world probably will be promoted vigorously, and it may well become part of the majority tradition.

Additionally, the new Convention will be less friendly to Anabaptist and progressive beliefs than the Convention was in the years leading up to 1979. This is unfortunate, as many of these beliefs seem to have exercised a good influence upon the Convention.

Here are a few examples. Even though most Baptists never accepted pacifism, the presence of that belief within the Convention probably served to curb aggressiveness.

Again, even though most Baptists did not accept the idea that justice is having decent food, clothing, housing, education, and job opportunities, the presence of that idea within the Convention served to alert many Baptists to the more ruthless side of capitalism.

Again, even though most Southern Baptists did not accept the idea that women may serve as pastors, the presence of that idea within the Convention had the effect of assisting many young women to take seriously the fact that they have spiritual gifts and that God may call them into his service.

Again, even though Baptists have been divided about whether or not Baptist higher education ought to include exploration and the questioning of tradition as well as the transmission of tradition, the presence within the Convention of a commitment to exploration helped the Convention to face up to the most serious sin in its history, namely, the injustice toward black people which had been a component in the life of the Southern Baptist Convention from its inception.

The new ecumenicity toward all Christians such as those who have spoken at recent Convention meetings, is encouraging but is hampered by the new restriction of ecumenism toward mainline Protestants, Catholics, and Orthodox.

Finally, it is possible though not yet clearly probable that two other clusters of beliefs may become part of the majority tradition in the new Convention. Calvinism may prevail, though it has an uphill battle. Parts of the deeper life understanding of Christian living may also prevail, and it is even possible that the entire understanding may be adopted.

The interpretation offered in the book is a personal one, as all interpretations are, and in these two last chapters I have mentioned my positive evaluation of the way we were theologically in the years leading up to 1979 and my negative evaluation of the changes in the new Convention. I do not intend now to make an extended plea for my readers to accept those evaluations. The Convention has decided collectively its general direction, and I accept that as a settled matter. Because I still have so very much in common with the new direction—the twenty-three beliefs of the majority tradition, especially the universal Christian beliefs—I am very happy to continue to be a part of the Convention. I believe that many others feel as I do about this.

But I do want to close with a question. It is the question which Governor Reagan made famous in his 1980 debate with President Carter. The question to Southern Baptists is: Are you better off than you were before 1979?

Many fine Southern Baptists feel that they are much better off. They believe that a course correction was needed, that a proper one has been made, and that the Convention can now proceed on the course it should have been following all along.

I do not believe this. I believe that the loss of the Protestant belief in the priesthood of all believers is unfortunate and that the loss of the distinctively Baptist beliefs in congregational decision-making by democratic means, in the careful separation of church and state, and in the rejection of all creeds but the Bible, are theological tragedies as great as any in the history of the Convention.

I also believe that the adoption of the three new beliefs—a militant resistance to liberalism, the inerrancy of the non-extant Hebrew and Greek manuscripts of the Bible in all matters including science and history as well as faith and practice, and the dispensational form of pre-millennial eschatology—does not represent very much gain for Southern Baptists. The destructive effects of an ongoing militancy are very worrisome. The call for affirmations concerning non-extant Hebrew and Greek texts of the Bible has the advantage of affirming vigorously the truthfulness of God, but its help is theoretical rather than practical. In practical terms, it does not add anything to the longstanding Baptist loyalty to the texts and translations we have and by which we must attempt to live as faithful Christians. Dispensational premillennialism is fascinating, but, insofar as being able to live in hope is concerned, it does not add anything helpful to the traditional Baptist view that "God, in His own time and in His own way, will bring the world to its appropriate end."

So, for me, this story is one of sadness. Others are persuaded that things are going to be much better for Southern Baptists in the future than they were in the years leading up to 1979. I pray that they are right and I am wrong. "Man proposes, but God disposes."[98]

Notes

¹*In necessariis unitas, in non necessariis libertas, in omnibus caritas.* Rupertus Meldenius, *Paranaenesis Votiva pro Pace Ecclesiae* (Rottenburg, 1626), p. 62. "Rupertus Meldenius" is the pseudonym for an orthodox Lutheran theologian, probably Peter Meiderlin who died in Augsburg in 1651. Philip Schaff called the these words "the motto of Christian Irenics." See Philip Schaff, *History of the Christian Church* (Grand Rapids: Wm. B. Eerdmans Publishing Company, 1974 [1910]), VII, pp. 650-652. See also Carl Bertheau, "Meldenius, Rupertus" in *The New Schaff-Herzog Encyclopedia of Religious Knowledge* edited by Samuel Macauley Jackson, VII (Grand Rapids: Baker Book House, 1968), p. 287.

Introduction

²Baylor, Richmond, Wake Forest, and Stetson are no longer completely controlled by their state Baptist conventions.

³The phrase apparently originated in the Churches of Christ, but it has been widely used by Southern Baptists for more than a century. Those who organized the Southern Baptist Convention in 1845 explained that they were not going to propose a creed for the new Convention because of the "Baptist aversion to all creeds." See William L. Lumpkin, "The Nature and Authority of Baptist Confessions of Faith," *Review and*

Expositor (Winter 1979), p. 25.

⁴Throughout this book I shall use the word "Baptists" to refer to Southern Baptists. The context will make it clear if I intend anyone other than Southern Baptists.

⁵To date, the churches have studied the doctrines of God, human beings, salvation, missions, the church, the family, biblical authority, the Holy Spirit, Christ, the laity, prayer, the priesthood of believers, creation, Lordship, and the Bible. In 1990 there was a summary study entitled *The Doctrines Baptists Believe* which comprised the doctrines of Scripture, God, human beings, the person of Christ, the work of Christ, salvation, the Christian life, the Spirit, the church, and last things.

⁶The books are on Christian doctrine, Jesus Christ, Scripture, God, creation, human beings, sin, the work and experience of salvation, the Holy Spirit, Christian living, the nature, life and mission of the church, hope, and Christian apologetics.

⁷In the twentieth century the list would include E. Y. Mullins, W. T. Conner, W. O. Carver, Frank Stagg, W. W. Stevens, Dale Moody, Dallas Roark, James Wm. McClendon, and Morris Ashcraft, to name only a few. For a review of the work of Baptist theologians, see *Baptist Theologians* edited by David S. Dockery and Timothy George (Nashville: Broadman Press, 1991).

⁸They are *Faith and Mission, Review and Expositor, Southwestern Journal of Theology,* and *The Theological Educator.*

⁹The Historical Commission of the Southern Baptist Convention publishes a journal entitled *Baptist History and Heritage* which includes a stream of articles about Baptist theologians.

¹⁰See Paul Basden, editor, *Has Our Theology Changed? Southern Baptist Thought Since 1845* (Nashville: Broadman Press, 1993). One criticism made of professional theologians during the controversy is that they were, in fact, too responsive to the academic discipline of theology and too little responsive to the churches.

[11]Nancy Tatom Ammerman, *Baptist Battles: Social Change and Religious Conflict in the Southern Baptist Convention* (New Brunswick: Rutgers University Press, 1990).

[12]*Foxfire 7* (Garden City: Anchor Books, 1973, 1980, 1982) edited by Paul F. Gillespie contains interviews with several Southern Baptist pastors in Appalachia. *The Theological Educator,* the journal of New Orleans Baptist Theological Seminary, published a series of interviews with Southern Baptist laypersons, pastors, missionaries, denominational leaders, and professors, on the topic of "Southern Baptist Theology Today," beginning in 1976. Other Southern Baptist leaders have been interviewed in newspapers and magazines.

[13]The need for multiple interpretations informs a book edited by Nancy Tatom Ammerman, *Southern Baptists Observed: Multiple Perspectives on a Changing Denomination* (Knoxville: University of Tennessee Press, 1993).

[14]Ellen M. Rosenberg, *The Southern Baptists: A Subculture in Transition* (Knoxville: The University of Tennessee Press, 1989).

[15]Claude L. Howe, Jr., has written two excellent articles which summarize the events in the controversy; they are "From Houston to Dallas" and "From Dallas to New Orleans" and they were published in *The Theological Educator* (Spring 1990). The best book interpreting the controversy historically, in my judgment, is *God's Last and Only Hope: The Fragmentation of the Southern Baptist Convention* by Bill J. Leonard (Grand Rapids: William B. Eerdmans, 1990). A very influential background study is "The 1980-81 Carver-Barnes Lectures" by Walter B. Shurden (Wake Forest: Southeastern Baptist Theological Seminary, 1980). For a history of the development of moderate institutions, see Walter B. Shurden, editor, *The Struggle for the Soul of the SBC* (Macon, Georgia: Mercer University Press, 1993); in it Shurden provides a summary of the major events in the controversy.

[16]In my judgment, the best sociological interpretation of the controversy is *Baptist Battles: Social Change and Religious Conflict*

in the Southern Baptist Convention by Nancy Tatom Ammerman.

[17]Many books tell about the personalities in the controversy. The indispensable insider's view is *What Happened to the Southern Baptist Convention?: A Memoir of the Controversy* by Grady C. Cothen (Macon, Georgia: Smyth & Helwys Publishing, 1993). James C. Hefley began in 1986 a series of books entitled *The Truth in Crisis* (Hannibal, Missouri: Hannibal Books, 1986 seq.) which is full of information about personalities and events. Joe Edward Barnhart's *The Southern Baptist Holy War: The Self-Destructive Struggle for Power within the Largest Protestant Denomination in America* (Austin: Texas Monthly Press, 1986) has some valuable vignettes. The cast of players is described in *The Takeover in the Southern Baptist Convention* edited by Rob James (Decatur, Georgia: SBC Today, 1989). Both the church press and the public press have carried hundreds of stories about the controversy; *SBC Today,* now called *Baptists Today,* is especially helpful. See also David Morgan, "Upheaval in the Southern Baptist Convention, 1979-1990, The Texas Connection," *Perspectives in Religious Studies* (Spring 1992).

[18]One of the most exhaustive studies of religion ever made is called "The Fundamentalism Project." The first book produced by that project is Martin E. Marty and R. Scott Appleby, editors, *Fundamentalisms Observed* (Chicago: University of Chicago Press, 1991).

[19]A recent history of the theology of the Southern Baptists is *Winds of Doctrines: The Origin and Development of Southern Baptist Theology* (Lanham, Maryland: University Press of America, 1991) by W. Wiley Richards. Richards offers a fascinating proposal that the theology of the Southern Baptists began as Calvinistic evangelicalism, became in the nineteenth century ecclesiastical evangelicalism, from 1900 to 1960 was evangelistic evangelicalism, and since 1960 has been engaged in a struggle to see whether it will continue as neo-orthodox evangelicalism or

as inerrancy evangelicalism. With much of this I agree, though the issue since 1960, it seems to me, might be better expressed as whether Southern Baptists will continue as evangelistic/missionary evangelicals or be transformed into inerrancy evangelicals; and the transformation is decidedly under way.

[20]The chairman of the committee which revised *The Baptist Faith and Message* in 1963, Herschel H. Hobbs, has written a commentary on the document, and, like that document, it is entitled *The Baptist Faith and Message* (Nashville: Convention Press, 1971). *What Southern Baptists Believe* (Louisville: Park Hurst Publishers, 1988) by Hankins Parker is also a running commentary on the theological themes developed in *The Baptist Faith and Message.*

[21]"The Southern Baptist Alliance Covenant" seems to have been designed to emphasize, among other things, distinctively Baptist beliefs. This is the confessional document of The Southern Baptist Alliance, now called The Alliance of Baptists. See Alan Neely, editor, *Being Baptist Means Freedom* (Charlotte: Southern Baptist Alliance, 1988).

[22]The sequence might have been done differently. I might have described revivalist beliefs before distinctively Baptist beliefs because the Baptists are a smaller unit within the larger revivalist group. I decided to follow the chronological sequence in Part One because it is necessary to employ the chronological sequence in Part Two.

Chapter 1

[23]Isaiah 40-66 is explicitly monotheistic; see, for example, 45:5.

[24]Blaise Pascal, *Pensées,* 131, translated by A. J. Krailsheimer (London: Penguin Books, 1966), p. 65.

[25]Other Baptists are more familiar with the Apostles' Creed. For example, Alexander Maclaren of Great Britain led the Baptist World Alliance to stand together and recite the Apostles'

Creed at its first meeting in London in 1905.

[26]See, for example, Joel 2 and Luke 11:11-13.

[27]Quoted in Albert McClellan, *Meet Southern Baptists* (Nashville: Broadman Press, 1978), pp. 29-30.

[28]Christ commands the church to baptize in Matthew 28:19-20, and to observe the Lord's Supper in Matthew 26:26-27. Luke tells of the first church doing these two things in Acts 2:41-42.

[29]Vincent of Lerins, "Commonitorium," II, 3: *"Quod semper, quod ubique, quod ab omnibus, creditum est."* See George E. McCracken and Allen Cabaniss, editors, *Early Medieval Theology* (Philadelphia: The Westminster Press, 1957), p. 38.

[30]A case can be made that there are a few beliefs which the entire church has held, which Southern Baptists do not hold. For example, Southern Baptists do not share the devotion which many Christians give to Mary. They resist Episcopal church order and the sacramentalism which developed early in the church's life. They reject the Constantinian settlement with its understanding that the government should support the church. Most of them do not accept the understanding of predestination which was proposed by Augustine and was accepted by Luther and Calvin. A case can be made that these beliefs are intrinsically necessary to Christian orthodoxy, but unless that is done, then Southern Baptists are orthodox Christians.

Chapter 2

[31]Romans 12:3-8, Revelation 21:9, I Peter 2:9.

[32]Currently four phrases are in use among Southern Baptists for the issue with which we are dealing here. They are "perseverance of the saints," "preservation of the saints," "the security of the believer," and "once saved, always saved." In using the word "secure," I am not opting for the superiority of that term to any of the others. For a criticism of some of the phrases, see Dale Moody, *The Word of Truth* (Grand Rapids: William B.

Eerdmans Publishing Company, 1981), pp. 361-362.

[33]See, for example, Romans 12:1 and Hebrews 13:15-16.

Chapter 3

[34]Earlier in the church's history, some other groups had renounced baptism, but none of them has survived as a church.

[35]There are only three hymns about baptism in the Baptist Hymnal, and they are found on pp. 242-244.

[36]Knowledgeable writers employ three phrases for the baptism of believers: "believer's baptism," "believers' baptism," and "believers baptism." The same is true of a church of believers, which is called by informed writers "believer's church," "believers' church," and "believers church." I have chosen the third usage in each instance because I see no need for a possessive in either case.

[37]Martin E. Marty, "Baptistification Takes Over," *Christianity Today* (September 2, 1983), p. 33.

[38]Max Weber called forms such as these "ideal types." See Max Weber, *Essays in Sociology,* translated by H. H. Gerth and C. Wright Mills (New York: Oxford University Press, 1946), pp. 323-324. Peter Berger says that the construction of ideal types is indispensable for understanding large and diverse fields of data; see Peter Berger, *The Heretical Imperative* (Garden City: Anchor Books, 1979), pp. 60-61.

[39]Eduard Schweizer, *Church Order in the New Testament* translated by Frank Clarke (London: SCM Press Ltd., 1961), p. 13.

[40]Quoted in Albert McClellan, *Meet Southern Baptists,* pp. 29-30.

[41]See, for example, Peter Berger et al., *The Homeless Mind* (London: Penguin Books, 1973), Chapter 2.

[42]William R. Estep, Jr., "Religious Freedom" (Nashville: The Historical Commission of the Southern Baptist Convention, 1989).

[43]A photocopy of the dedication may be seen in Albert McClellan, *Meet Southern Baptists,* p. 12. I have provided modern spelling for the quotation.

[44]Quoted in Edwin S. Gaustad, *Liberty of Conscience: Roger Williams in America* (Grand Rapids: William B. Eerdmans Publishing Company, 1991), p. 146.

[45]George W. Truett, "Baptists and Religious Liberty" (Nashville: The Sunday School Board of the Southern Baptist Convention, n.d.), p. 26.

[46]An alternative to the interpretation offered here is that the distinction between prescriptive creeds and descriptive confessions was not prominent until the twentieth century, and that earlier Baptists employed creeds prescriptively as long as they were voluntary and non-coercive, and especially, not sanctioned by the state. See Timothy George, "Conflict and Identity in the SBC" in *Beyond the Impasse?: Scripture, Interpretation, and Theology in Baptist Life* edited by Robison B. James and David S. Dockery (Nashville: Broadman Press, 1992), pp. 202-207.

[47]William L. Lumpkin, Baptist Confessions of Faith (Philadelphia: Judson Press, 1959), p. 16.

[48]Letter from Helen Jean Parks and R. Keith Parks, to all foreign missionaries of the Southern Baptist Convention, March 27, 1992, p. 2.

Chapter 4

[49]Two Southern Baptist historians, James Leo Garrett and E. Glenn Hinson, have debated whether it is proper to call Southern Baptists "evangelicals," a question which is relevant to the present chapter, for what I am calling "revivalism" is often referred to as "the evangelical revival." In my judgment, it is right to say that Southern Baptists are evangelicals inasmuch as they have been very influenced by the revivalist movement and share many things in common with the wider evangelical movement in America today, things such as a vigorous commitment

to evangelism. On the other hand, it is right to say that Southern Baptists are not evangelicals inasmuch as they existed prior to the revivalist movement and they have distinctive beliefs and practices such as believers baptism which must be set aside in order to participate in the evangelical movement in America which includes Methodists, for example. See James Leo Garrett, E. Glenn Hinson, and James E. Tull, *Are Southern Baptists "Evangelicals"?* (Macon, Georgia: Mercer University Press, 1983). For an illustration of the fact that the revivalist tradition is the center of gravity for many Southern Baptists, notice that the first chapter of a recent book by William Tuck emphasizes religious experience and evangelism, and links these to believers baptism and a believers church. William Powell Tuck, *Our Baptist Tradition* (Macon, Georgia: Smyth & Helwys Publishing, Inc., 1933), Chapter 1.

[50]John Wesley, Journal, entry for May 15, 1738. John W. Drakeford, editor, *John Wesley* (Nashville: Broadman Press, 1979), p. 62.

[51]Quoted in Albert McClellan, *Meet Southern Baptists,* pp. 29-30.

Chapter 5

[52]Ernst Troelsch, *The Social Teaching of the Christian Churches* translated by Olive Wyon (New York: Macmillan Publishing Company, 1931), I, 331ff..

[53]Edward L. Queen, *In The South the Baptists Are the Center of Gravity: Southern Baptists and Social Change, 1930-1980* (Brooklyn: Carlson Publishing Inc, 1991).

Chapter 6

[54]See Philip Schaff, *The Creeds of Christendom.* III, *The Evangelical Protestant Creeds,* fourth edition (New York: Harper and Brothers, 1919), pp. 550-597.

[55]For the case that Baptists are more closely aligned with the

magisterial Reformation than is suggested here, see Timothy George, "The Reformation Roots of the Baptist Tradition" in *Review and Expositor* (Winter, 1989), pp. 9-22.

[56]A milder version of this is single predestination, which says that God predestinated some to be saved and did not predestinate others. The end result of the two views is the same. Calvinism completely rejects the suggestion that predestination follows God's foreknowledge.

[57]For examples of each, see Hebrews 9:1-14, Colossians 2:15, I John 4:9, and I Peter 2:21.

[58]Walter Shurden, "The 1980-81 Carver-Barnes Lectures" (Wake Forest: Southeastern Baptist Theological Seminary, 1980).

[59]John Loftis, *Factors in Southern Baptist Identity as Reflected by Ministerial Role Models,* 1750-1925 (Unpublished doctoral dissertation, Southern Baptist Theological Seminary, 1987).

Chapter 7

[60]Leon McBeth, *The Baptist Heritage* (Nashville: Broadman Press, 1987), p. 60.

[61]Leon McBeth, *The Baptist Heritage,* p. 68.

Chapter 8

[62]W. E. Boardman, *The Higher Christian Life* (Boston: Henry Hoyt, 1859).

[63]Jack R. Taylor, *The Key to Triumphant Living* (Nashville: Broadman Press, 1971).

[64]Quoted in Daniel G. Reid et al., editors, *Dictionary of Christianity in America* (Downers Grove: InterVarsity Press, 1990), p. 1096.

[65]Jack R. Taylor, *The Key to Triumphant Living,* p. 27.

[66]See Jack R. Taylor, *The Key to Triumphant Living,* p. 16.

Chapter 9

[67]Note the respect with which Machen is treated by that least religious of American social critics, Walter Lippmann, in *The Preface to Morals* (New York: The Macmillan Company, 1929), pp. 31-34. Mark Noll reviews the change of leadership in fundamentalism in *Between Faith and Criticism: Evangelicals, Scholarship, and the Bible in America* (San Francisco: Harper & Row, 1986).

[68]Ernest Sandeen, *The Roots of Fundamentalism* (Chicago: University of Chicago Press, 1970).

[69]George Marsden, *Fundamentalism and American Culture* (Oxford University Press, 1980).

[70]George W. Dollar, *A History of Fundamentalism in America* (Greenville: Bob Jones University Press, n.d.). The definition appears in large, bold type on an unnumbered page before the text of the book begins.

[71]"The Chicago Statement on Biblical Inerrancy" (Walnut Creek, California: The International Council on Biblical Inerrancy, n.d. [1978]).

[72]See Robison B. James, editor, *The Unfettered Word: Southern Baptists Confront the Authority-Inerrancy Question* (Waco: Word Books, 1987); L. Russ Bush and Tom J. Nettles, *Baptists and the Bible* (Chicago: Moody Press, 1980); Michael Smith, editor, *The Proceedings of the Conference on Biblical Inerrancy* (Nashville: Broadman Press, 1987); and David S. Dockery and Philip D. Wise, "Biblical Inerrancy: Pro or Con?" in *The Theological Educator* (Spring 1988), pp. 15-44.

[73]David S. Dockery, *The Doctrine of the Bible* (Nashville: Convention Press, 1991).

Chapter 10

[74]H. Leon McBeth, *Women in Baptist Life* (Nashville: Broadman Press, 1979).

[75]For details, see Juliette Mather, "Women, Convention

Privileges of" in *Encyclopedia of Southern Baptists* (Nashville: Broadman Press, 1958) II, 1542-44.

[76]The first woman...in 1963: See Catherine B. Allen, "Women's Movements and Southern Baptists" in *Encyclopedia of Southern Baptists* (Nashville: Broadman Press, 1982) IV, 2560-2562.

[77]See C. Anne Davis, "Women, Ordination of Southern Baptist" in *Encyclopedia of Southern Baptists,* IV, 2557-2558. The Watts Street Baptist Church of Durham, North Carolina, ordained Addie Davis on August 9, 1964.

[78]Charlene Kaemmerling, "Ordination of Women: Wrong or Right?" in *The Theological Educator* (Spring 1988), pp. 98-99.

[79]See Marjorie Warkentin, *Ordination: A Biblical-Historical View* (Grand Rapids: William B. Eerdmans Publishing Company, 1982).

[80]"Southern Baptist Theology Today: An Interview with C. Penrose St. Amant" in *The Theological Educator* (Spring 1982), p. 16.

[81]Criticism is an essentially contested concept in the church today. The present proposal draws upon a presentation by R. G. Collingwood in *The Idea of History* (Oxford University Press, 1956), pp. 269-270. For the idea of an essentially contested concept, see W. B. Gallie, *Philosophy and the Historical Understanding* (New York: Schocken Books, 1964), pp. 157ff.

[82]See Stephen Neill, *The Interpretation of the New Testament, 1861-1961* (London: Oxford University Press, 1966), pp. 315ff. Neill tells how the orthodox Jewish scholar, Dr. Israel Abrahams, who was Reader in Rabbinics at Cambridge, startled a learned society by remarking that "to us Jews the Fourth Gospel is the most Jewish of the four."

[83]Andrew Louth, *Discerning the Mystery: An Essay on the Nature of Theology* (Oxford: Clarendon Press, 1983), Chapter V. Louth now teaches in London.

Chapter 11

[84]C. H. Dodd, "A Letter concerning Unavowed Motives in Ecumenical Discussions" in *The Ecumenical Review* (Autumn 1949), pp. 52-56.

[85]This quotation is from the document which was distributed to messengers at the Convention in 1988. The document formally affirms the priesthood of all believers, but it suggests that the importance of that belief had been exaggerated by some of the old leaders.

[86]"Report of the Southern Baptist Convention Peace Committee," *SBC Bulletin* (St. Louis, June 16, 1987), p. 12.

[87]Ibid., p. 14.

[88]Walter B. Shurden, *The Baptist Identity: Four Fragile Freedoms* (Macon, Georgia: Smyth & Helwys Publishing, Inc., 1993), pp. 55-59. Shurden had insisted on the same point in his controversial earlier book, *The Doctrine of the Priesthood of Believers* (Nashville: Convention Press, 1987).

[89]William Powell Tuck, *Our Baptist Tradition* (Macon, Georgia: Smyth & Helwys Publishing, Inc., 1993), p. 64.

[90]Cecil E. Sherman, "Freedom of Individual Interpretation" in *Being Baptist Means Freedom* edited by Alan Neely (Charlotte: Southern Baptist Alliance, 1988), pp. 9-24.

[91]Walter Shurden believes that they will "pay for what they control." See Walter B. Shurden, editor, *The Struggle for the Soul of the SBC*, p. 283. I am not so sure.

[92]The Christian Life Commission filed a friend of the court brief in *Lee v. Weissman* in support of the offering of prayers at a public high school graduation.

[93]It is greatest in the years leading up to 1979. From the founding of the Convention in 1845 until the 1960s, the besetting sin of the Convention was identical to the besetting sin of the nation, the unjust treatment of black people.

Chapter 12

[94]See Paige Patterson, "Stalemate" in *The Theological Educator* (Special Issue, The Controversy in the SBC, 1985), pp. 7-8.

[95]See, for example, the interview with Adrian Rogers in *The Theological Educator* (Spring 1988), p. 9.

[96]See, for example, Jerry Vines, "Eschatology, Premillennial or Amillennial?" in *The Theological Educator* (Spring 1988), pp. 134-144.

[97]These four are all in some sense issues of freedom, and this confirms what other observers have said. See, for example, Walter B. Shurden, "Major Issues in the SBC Controversy" in *Amidst Babel, Speak the Truth: Reflections on the Southern Baptist Convention Struggle,* edited by Robert U. Ferguson, Jr. (Macon, Georgia: Smyth & Helwys Publishing, Inc., 1993), p. 4. In his book, *The Baptist Identity: Four Fragile Freedoms* (Macon, Georgia: Smyth & Helwys, 1993), Shurden argues that freedom is the single most important casualty in the new Convention.

[98]Thomas a Kempis, *The Imitation of Christ,* I, 19. See Morris Ashcraft, editor, *Medieval Christianity* (Nashville: Broadman Press, 1981), p. 390.

About The Author

FISHER HUMPHREYS is Professor of Theology at Beeson
Divinity School of Samford University in Birmingham.
He has been pastor of churches in Alabama, Illinois, and
Mississippi. He is a graduate of Mississippi College
(B.A.), New Orleans Baptist Theological Seminary (B.D.,
Th.D.), and Oxford University (M. Litt.). *The Way We
Were* is his sixth book.